COUNSELING YOU CAN

Trust

A practical aid to Christian counseling

Dr. Dawn Meng

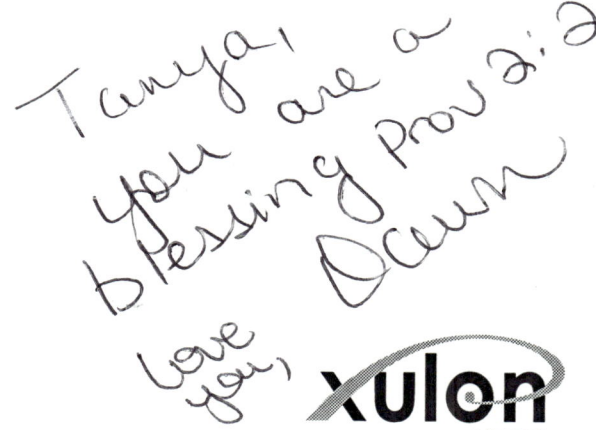

Tanya,
You are a blessing Prov 3:3
Love you,
Dawn

xulon PRESS

www.xulonpress.com

List of Contents

INTRODUCTION

Pastoral counseling is, in actuality, biblical counseling, and a pastoral counselor should be considered a part of church leadership. Furthermore, I conclude, based on years of experience, that true, effective pastoral counseling is *prophetic* pastoral counseling because it is the life of the *revealed* counsel from the Holy Spirit that produces true change in the counselee.

Many in the Church are suffering. These victims, however, often follow secular psychology when there is a lack of sound counseling and teaching in their church. Survivors of "trials and temptations" are those who hear the Word of God and do it (see John 8:31). The Bible calls these people disciples. Many in the Church need to be helped so that they may become disciples of Christ. The pastoral counselor is part of the answer, and the Lord wants to use the pastoral counselor to help snatch them out of the snare of the fowler.

The purpose of this book is three-fold: to give counselors and pastors more knowledge; to guide Christian professional counselors on a path back to biblical counseling; to teach the purpose of Jesus' life, death, and resurrection from a counseling perspective (see John 3:17-21, 10:10; Rom. 3:28).

I will not use statistics for two reasons: numbers can be manipulated to read whatever someone wants them to read; statistics change over time. Yet the Bible does not change (see Heb. 13:8). The Word of God is truth (see John 14:6; Eph. 4:21).

— Dr. Dawn Meng

CHAPTER 1

ACCOUNTABILITY

Ultimately we will be accountable for all our deeds done on earth (see Rom. 2:6). In James 5:16, God commands us to confess our sins one to another that we may be healed. Confession is the first principle of accountability — telling someone your sin or problem — and is the first step in conquering your sin or problem.

In God's Word there is complete divine healing and deliverance if you choose to "work out your salvation in fear and trembling" (Phil. 2:12). *Katergazomai* is the Greek word in this verse. It means to work out or to finish, implying a process. The Greek word for "salvation" is *soteria*, which means rescue (physically or morally). One can be delivered (or rescued) from a chemical substance, however, the root of the problem (usually rejection) often remains. It is the process of accountability that can be a very important ingredient in working out this recovery.

The most important issue regarding accountability is confronting self. "God holds you responsible for all our own deeds (thoughts, words, and actions), including those that are life-dominating or those that are thought to be 'genetically predisposed' or 'addictive'."[1] The thinking process is included in the definition of the word deeds. Sin begins in the thought life.

Proverbs 4:23 exhorts, "keep thy heart with all diligence; for out of it are the issues of life" (KJV). "Issues" in the Hebrew language is *towtsa'ah*. This word is used to refer to a geographical border or boundary. There is a correlation between accountability and establishing "borders."

In pastoral counseling, there are boundaries that must be given to the counselee in order for true, effective accountability to occur. An example is the role of the counselor in regard to the counselee. Distinct recognition of these two separate roles is important so that no emotional or physical enmeshment occurs. Emotional enmeshment can lead to sexual involvement at both the pastoral and the professional level.

As a missionary in Asia, I counseled a pastor's wife who had become so close to the nationals that she went to public baths with them. This opened the door for emotional enmeshment, which required intervention. I discerned that the missionary needed to have a healthy space between herself and the nationals and that she needed healing from a deep root of rejection. It took several weeks for her to recover, but God did it.

Secular counselors are more prone to be sexually bonded with a person other than a heterosexual spouse. I was a member of the California Association of Marriage and Family Therapists for almost nine years. Every quarterly publication of the professional magazine revealed members whose licenses were revoked or suspended and the reasons why, and it mentioned those who had been "caught in sexual sin." These counselors had failed the boundary test.

The key question in counseling situations is not only, "Do you want to change?" but also, "Are you willing to do whatever it takes in order for true change to occur?" The fact is that *all Christians* have begun the process of change since conversion (as a caterpillar changes into a butterfly). The Bible says, "Therefore if any person is [engrafted] in

Christ (the Messiah) he is a new creation (a new creature altogether); the old [previous moral and spiritual condition] has passed away. Behold, the fresh *and* new has come" (2 Cor. 5:17, AMP, italics added). Concerning change, Second Corinthians 3:18 says, "But we all, with open face beholding as in a glass the glory of the Lord, are changed into the same image from glory to glory, even as by the Spirit of the Lord" (KJV). The point is not only that we are being changed from glory to glory but also that we all must be "open face." In the Greek language, "open face" means either to be unveiled as a person or for the surface to be unveiled. This implies a revealing of self (thoughts, deeds, and words) in order to be properly changed from glory to glory. This metamorphosis comes by the Holy Spirit, the Great Counselor. Yet at the same time we need each other. That is why Jesus Christ placed under-shepherds in His Church — for the purpose of feeding and nurturing the flock, not for controlling it.

There is a big difference between accountability and control. The person who seeks to control apart from Jesus is manipulating. This leads us to the important point that the divine call of a pastoral counselor must be treated delicately because sheep are delicate. Admonition can only take place in the context of love and humility, for it requires the admonisher to first of all remove the log in his own eye in order to take out the splinter in another's.[2] Pastoral counselors with an effective ministry of accountability seek to release healed sheep. On the other hand those with a controlling spirit seek to keep the healed sheep as his or her possessions. True "pastors" practice Second Corinthians 1:4-5 (overflowing Christian love) on behalf of Christ's flock by freeing them. Yet controlling ones rarely determine a person to be "healed completely."

It takes a humble person to admit wrong *and* to submit to someone in an accountability relationship until he or she is restored. However, it must happen.

CHAPTER 2

ANGER AND BITTERNESS

The root of [anger] is "grief or trouble" caused by hurt

A + B — Signs of being self focused on self rather than God

Many people have said that depression is anger turned inward, but few people have attempted to define anger. The word means grief or trouble. I believe this is more accurate than the contemporary definition, which refers to anger as a strong feeling of displeasure. That's because at the root of most anger is hurt — caused by grief or trouble.

Anger and bitterness are two noticeable signs of being focused on self and not trusting God's sovereignty in your life.[3] This also could mean not trusting God that He has allowed your family circumstances for your betterment. Many who come for counseling often view a negative family circumstance as a detriment, and they may carry some painful excess "weight" — anger, bitterness.

John the Apostle, in his third epistle, writes to Gaius, "Dear friend, I pray that you may enjoy good health and that all may go well with you, even as your soul is getting along well" (3 John 2, NIV). It is interesting to see that "health" in Greek is *hugiaino*, meaning wholeness. Anger is related to physiological health. When I worked at a hospital for chemically dependent teens, the director educated us about some aspects of anger. He said that most anger is stored in three parts of the body: the head — in the form of headaches (usually migraine), the upper body — in the form of respiratory problems, and the abdominal area — in the form of ulcers and digestive problems.

headaches — respiratory — digestion

13

A lady who came to me for counseling was suffering from migraine headaches. I deducted in one of the sessions that her domineering, biological mother inappropriately handled her in a sexual manner. She was not in good health, and her soul was not prospering. In order for the headaches to disappear, she needed to forgive (see Matt. 6:14; Luke 23:34; Col. 3:13) and physiologically she needed to "express" her repressed anger. Secular therapy only takes into account the latter. A person can remove guilt from the conscious mind... but the guilt will remain in the subconscious area, causing... anger.[4] Her anger was a result of subconscious guilt. Untreated subconscious guilt can lead to spiritual and/or premature physical death, all because of a lack of self-confrontation.

Spiritually, anger and bitterness are like venom. In fact, *pikria*, the Greek word for "bitterness", refers to poison. Hebrews 12:15-16a admonishes us to "exercise foresight and be on the watch to look [after one another] to see that no one falls back from and fails to secure God's grace (His unmerited favor and spiritual blessing), in order that no root of resentment (rancor, bitterness, or hatred) shoot forth and cause trouble and bitter torment, and the many become contaminated and defiled by it; that no one may become guilty" (AMP).

How does guilt relate to anger and bitterness? Guilt can be called conviction. Adam and Eve were under conviction after they had sinned. They were naked and ashamed. Instead of owning their own wrong, they both began the cycle of blame shifting that is so detrimental to human relationships. One of the root causes of blame shifting is anger. This is also termed "transference" in secular therapy. Transference is the shift of emotions, especially those experienced in childhood (or adulthood), from one person or object to another, especially the transfer of feelings about a parent to an analyst.[5] I add to that definition, "transfer of feelings about a parent to a spouse", common in marriages. Many couples fall into sin when this type of emotional transference takes place.

Scripture describes adults relating to God and to each other (ex., the Psalms and Esther). A vital verse that warns fathers not to provoke their children to wrath is Ephesians 6:4. Wrath in this verse means anger. Why did God put this verse in the Bible if He did not know that fathers, much more than mothers, would need to concentrate on bringing children up in the nurture, education, and training of the Lord *without anger*? Most fathers have to work at being good instructors and disciplinarians because many did not have a good example at home in their own upbringing.

One husband and father I counseled was reared in a home full of violence and strife. His parents often attempted to assault one another. In one instance, he secured a weapon in order to prevent the fighting. When I met with him, he was not only experiencing real and imaginary physical pain, but he was also transferring the anger he had toward his parents onto his wife. He displayed violence through voice tone and punching holes in the walls. Furthermore he was bound by a sexual addiction that demanded he have sex up to several times daily.

The first time I met with him and his wife, I only knew a little about his violent background and his physical pain (secular psychotherapists term this the "presenting problem"). After the husband shared some superficial words about himself and his pain, I looked at him and said, "Before you came today, God told me your whole life story. Do you want to hear it?" "Of course," he replied. At that point, I read Hebrews 12:4-17:

Ye have not yet resisted unto blood, striving against sin. And ye have forgotten the exhortation which speaketh unto you as unto children. My son, despise not thou the chastening of the Lord, nor faint when thou art rebuked of him: For whom the Lord loveth he chasteneth, and scourgeth every son whom he receiveth. If ye endure chastening, God dealeth with you as with sons; for what son is he whom the father chasteneth not? But if ye be without chastisement, whereof all are partakers, then are ye bastards, and not sons. Furthermore we have had fathers of our flesh which corrected *us* and we gave them reverence: shall we not much rather be in subjection unto the Father of spirits, and live? For they verily for a few days chastened us after their own pleasure; but he for *our* profit, that *we* might be partakers of his holiness. Now no chastening for the present seemeth to be joyous, but grievous: nevertheless afterward it yieldeth the peaceable fruit of righteousness unto them which are exercised thereby. Wherefore lift up the hands which hang down, and the feeble knees; and make straight paths for your feet, lest that which is lame be turned out of the way; but let it rather be healed. Follow peace with all *men*, and holiness, without which no man shall see the Lord: Looking diligently lest any man fail of the grace of God; lest any root of bitterness springing up trouble *you*, and thereby many be defiled; Lest there *be* any fornicator, or profane person, as Esau, who for one morsel of meat sold his birthright. For ye know how that afterward, when he would have inherited the blessing, he was rejected: for he found no place of repentance, though he sought it carefully with tears (KJV, italics added).

He continued to tell me about pain *in his knee* for which he was taking addictive painkillers with no results. I said, "You must forgive *whomever* offended you," and I reread verse 17.

The real problem was that he had not fully repented at the time of his conversion. Now some would say this man was not even "saved" because he did not willfully accept the Lord but made only an emotional decision. I counseled him as if he were saved though not properly trained, in order to be more pastoral. No one responds favorably to judgment. However the Bible says to confront the unruly — the impulsive addicts. In the Greek language, this word is *ataktos*, which means disorderly. Most addicts display their anger quite well in public. Unfortunately it is in the church that much anger is hidden from view and appears in other forms, such as emotional and sexual abuse, eating disorders, subjective preaching, and neglect of children.

The first significant question I always ask in therapy is, "How is your devotional life on a daily basis?" My second question is similar: "Are you praying regularly?" Usually the answer is a negative one to one or both questions. Why do I ask these questions? Anger against God or man hinders intimacy with the Lord. "For the anger of man does not achieve the righteousness of God" (James 1:20, NAS). A sure sign of anger is murmuring, which God does not approve of. To murmur because of the hardness of the way, to complain about our circumstance, is to actually murmur against God. To murmur is to stop the flow of God's creative power. Instead of multiplying our resources, we tend to lose even that which we thought we had.[6]

There was a certain wife who, for the first six months of her marriage, was murmuring against God. She was a virgin when she married. Her husband was not, though for nearly ten years he had been pure before God after his conversion. Unknown to the husband was a venereal disease that he had acquired in his late teens but had lain dormant in his body for years. It was not long after the wedding that the woman began experiencing physical pain. When she medically discovered that she had contracted the disease, the wife began to murmur and complain, not only against her husband but against God also. Even though she knew that she needed to thank God in *all* things (James 1:2), praising God in the midst of *this* thing was difficult. After a season of murmuring, she began to counsel herself, asking, "What would I tell someone in my situation?" She then realized this situation was not God's fault. Furthermore it impacted her of the reality of how a background of faithfulness can benefit a person's life, as well as the consequences of sin may eventually cause harm, even harm to innocent others. She learned the biblical truth that often "God's method of bringing us into maturity of love is through suffering and affliction."[7]

This woman can now relate very well to someone who has been though the emotional pain of adultery because, in effect, those were the dynamics that took place concerning her. There will be anger involved in these types of situations, but God cannot use a bitter vessel. He *will* use a broken vessel and one who has practiced forgiveness. Angry people must forgive (see Matt. 5:21-22). The Bible several times commands to forgive, and *then* we will be forgiven. That is a challenging paradox for most people, especially those who come in for counseling.

People who are angry usually want to blame others first. People who are depressed (inward anger) usually blame themselves. In some Christian circles people say, "I'm mad at the devil." But if we are saying *that*, then we are still mad (possessing wrath). It is, however, indirectly biblical to be "mad at the devil." What then are we to do? No doubt, Satan has come to steal, kill, and destroy (see John 10:10), but regarding anger, Paul commands us to "put it away" (obey Col. 3:8). The Greek word is *apotithemi*, meaning to cast off, implying that "deliverance" needs to take place.

[margin handwritten note: God can use a broken vessel, but won't use a bitter vessel.]

Once I had a counseling session with a mother and her five year-old daughter who had been molested. The little girl was displaying anger through disrespect and hyperactivity. At a very early age, she was headed down the path of rebellion and destruction. Since anger is stored in the body, it can be released though healthy, physical activity (that is why worldly techniques like hypno-therapy, breathing exercises, biofeedback, and primal therapy work for a season, but they are not effective for long-term healing because the root of unforgiveness has not been dealt with). I ministered the principle of prayer and forgiveness with the language of a five year old. Then I took an empty tissue box and asked her to pretend that it was the devil. "Kick it as far across the room as you can," I said. She did so very aggressively. Finally, she stepped on it, making it completely flat.

In every following session that I included a healthy, physical activity, the counselee went away feeling physically better instead of drained. The reason this little girl felt better is because exercising physical strength releases endorphins in the brain, which not strangely enough is similar to the drug morphine used in medicine to dull pain. God Himself gave us wonderful methods in His Word to express ourselves physically in order to stay healthy, thus not giving anger a foothold in our lives. More than thirteen times the Bible tells us to shout unto God. Never does it mention yelling at the devil. The original meaning of rejoice, when David rejoiced in the Lord's salvation, is to spin around with emotion.

Even the words "violence" and "force" in Matthew 11:12 have been misinterpreted by some well-meaning Christians as yelling and screaming at the devil. However, these two words come from the same Greek word that is used in Acts 8:39 to describe the translation of Philip the Evangelist. Furthermore, if it were necessary to raise one's voice to take the "kingdom of God by force", then China would not be experiencing one of the greatest outpourings of the Holy

endorphines released — are similar during exercise — dulling pain to morphine

Word says shout to the Lord not yell at the devil!

Rejoice - spin around 19 with emotion

Spirit of all time. Certain groups of Chinese Christians meet secretly and quietly at night to worship Christ in order that they will not be discovered.

When I have counseled battered women, I have never suggested that they go around the house commanding the devil to "come out" of their husbands, though their husbands may indeed be demonized. It is the kindness of the Lord that leads them to repentance, even though earnest, consistent intercession is often needed. Most of all, they must have reliance on and trust in Jesus who lives to make intercession for them. I have discovered that battered women (those in an anger-filled environment) must use the time when their husbands are calm as a gentle ministry and affectionate time to them. Husbands' hearts will become softer and more open to the love they rarely received in their childhood. Life-changing results have occurred when wives also realize their role as an emotional helpmate, rather than merely a domestic one.

Another unhealthy and unholy expression of anger comes in the form of child abuse. Child abuse includes neglect, sexual abuse, and physical abuse, all legally punishable in various degrees. In the United States, we have the strictest laws in the world concerning child abuse, yet some of the weakest methods in dealing with the real issues. As a society, we have lost the meaning of the verse spoken by Cain in Genesis 4:9, "Am I my brother's keeper?" He was manifesting a fruit of anger — neglect. He was sowing seeds of rebellion, and finally ended up leaving the presence of the Lord.

What are needed are pastoral counselors of understanding. We must once again teach our congregations the art of loving and caring. Home groups are an excellent way to see this become a reality (see Acts 2:46), not only for practical support but for spiritual support also. From the pulpit we must also be willing and able to share personal triumphs *and* defeats in order to encourage others to self-disclose within the context of small groups.

The TV/VCR/Internet and double-income era has exponentially increased the number of emotionally, spiritually, and physically neglected children. Fathers, including clergy, have been seriously at fault for neglecting their own heritage. Finding balance between work and ministry to family has been a major problem in the church for years. Some "ministers" of the Gospel take Matthew 19:29 out of context and literally "forsake" their wives and children by alienating them and even divorcing them altogether for the "sake of the ministry", when the Bible clearly states, "For if a man does not know how to rule his own household, how is he to take care of the church of God?" (1 Tim. 3:5, AMP).

More fear of (reverence for) God and less fear of man will certainly decrease one's carnal "right" to be angry. Paul, in his letter to the Ephesians, gives permission to be angry as long as one does not sin — not giving place to the devil (see 4:26-27). Unrighteous anger is the repercussion of breaking down interpersonal boundaries. Righteous anger can turn into unrighteous anger if the feeling leads one to sinful actions or causes one to want to punish the person(s) with whom he or she is angry. If you harbor anger, anger will turn into bitterness, only to defile many. However unrighteous anger is dissipated when you yield "right of ownership" or "right of judgment" to the Lord. For example, King David's justifiable anger against Nabal was transferred to the righteous judge of Nabal, the Lord (1 Sam. 25:28-31).

The person struggling with anger needs revelatory ideas. Many have already tried dealing with their anger by counting to ten, leaving the room, sending the child to his or her room, or taking a drive in the car. I have often prescribed

[handwritten marginal note, right margin: Harboring anger turns it into bitterness + defiles others as well. Unrighteous anger is the repercussion of breaking down interpersonal boundaries.]

21

praise and worship, reading or copying verses of the Bible in longhand, or going to a secluded room for prayer as "homework" for the person with a root of anger. A concrete plan for accountability is enacted as well; he or she is asked at the next meeting how his or her new life is progressing.

CHAPTER 3

BEAUTY

*But the Lord said to Samuel, "Do not look at his
appearance or at the height of his stature, because I
have rejected him; for God sees not as man sees, for
man looks at the outward appearance, but the Lord
looks at the heart"* (1 Sam. 16:7, NAS).

A sister in Christ who conducted beauty and personality
seminars once quoted to me the above verse, and then
said, "Dawn, God does know your heart. Man does not, so *he*
looks at the appearance." Her statement is so true. People so
easily judge others by the outward appearance — the clothes
they wear, the cars they drive, the neighborhoods they live
in, the schools they attend, etc. God does not and never will
look on our appearance; He always looks at the heart — the
source of our motives and drives.

Beauty in the eyes of the Lord is a difficult concept for
many young people to cleave to. Clothes, cosmetics, and
materialism have swept many of our youth into the "lust of
the flesh, the lust of the eyes, and the pride of life." Correct
attitudes, motives, and character, however, are what truly
make a person beautiful.

An activity that greatly influenced my life as an adolescent (a crucial time in regard to beauty) was when I attended
a youth event called "Turning Point", conducted by a local
church. The leaders were aware of the emotional needs of

adolescents. They planned for each encounter candidate to receive a loving letter from his or her parent(s) or legal guardian(s). After I read the letter from my mother, I was emotionally touched. Her words included, "You are like a beautiful blooming rose; you have always been in God's hands from the time of your birth. I love you very much." After this retreat (better to call it "advance"!), our family began to assist in these youth retreats over the next five years. My brother attended his first retreat after I did. During a break at one retreat, he told me with brotherly love, "Dawn, I think you are beautiful." Until that time, I really did not think I was physically beautiful (only inwardly beautiful due to the Lord's salvation), but I knew his words were sincere. The impact was long lasting in our sibling relationship.

My father wrote in my high school yearbook during my senior year, "Dawn, many daughters have done nobly, but you excel them all. Love, Mom and Dad" (Prov. 31:29, NAS). They were words from his heart, and they impacted my life.

An important point regarding ministry to teens is that pastoral counselors must encourage them with the Word of God concerning inner beauty, especially young women. The Bible says in First Timothy 2:9-10, "I also want women to dress modestly, with decency and propriety, not with braided hair or gold or pearls or expensive clothes, but with good deeds, appropriate for women who profess to worship God" (NIV). It is significant that the Bible contains this verse because many young women lack encouragement from their fathers to excel inwardly. Young women who lack healthy attention and affirmation from their fathers end up, in some way or another, seeking it from other males at a time when they are so emotionally and physically vulnerable.

I saw this reality in hundreds of teens that came into a Crisis Pregnancy Center where I once counseled. In particular, a young teen named Michelle came one day. She was fourteen and possibly on her second pregnancy. She had no father present in her home or any fatherly image in her life. Men had used and abused her. Her first child was in the care of a relative. Two months prior to her visit, her own mother had filed for bankruptcy. Michelle came to me openly thinking that her only "way out" was suicide. I remained calm and called the director of an unwed mother's home in order to try to get the client in a safe place for the night (good counselors do not panic in suicide situations). The director and I began to ask her what she "intended to do" regarding her suicidal plans. She was convincing. I realized I needed an encouraging word from the Holy Spirit to move her toward a relationship with Christ. It was my tendency to quote John 3:16 or John 10:10 in these types of situations. Instead, I quoted Psalm 127:3a, "Children are a heritage from the Lord." The client began to weep. I explained to her about the beautiful aspects of motherhood — about Mary the mother of Jesus and about Elizabeth the mother of John the Baptist. She aborted her plans to commit suicide, moved into the unwed mother's home, and was lovingly guided into a body of believers that loved and cared for her. Her first experience with receiving love and with being affirmed of her inner beauty was in this home.

It is no small wonder that physical beauty has been significant in society for thousands of years. Therefore it is imperative that pastoral counselors have the "mind of Christ" concerning the concept of inner beauty. Pastoral counselors must pray earnestly in the prayer closet in order to "see" counselees with supernatural, Christ-like eyes and minds rather than just what they see on the outside. Pastoral counselors are called to be God's ambassadors (2 Cor. 5:20) for the kingdom of heaven on behalf of others.

People have often said, "Beauty is in the eye of the beholder." That was spoken from human, natural terms, but pastoral counselors must learn to behold people through the eyes of His Spirit. Pastoral counselors must begin to see the inner potential in each and every person encountered in the counseling ministry. They must not *focus* on the external condition nor the symptoms of the individual, but on the internal person and on the goal of all counseling, summed up in Second Corinthians 1:3-7 and Ephesians 3:16-19. Almost everyone without fail will naturally want to focus on the external and on the symptoms. It is good to listen with cognitive understanding, but eventually pastoral counselors should begin to operate in the supernatural realm of the Holy Spirit. For example, one may say things like, "I sense (not *know*) that you are depressed, but let us not focus on your depression. Let us focus on what God can do for others through your experience." When words like this are spoken, it plants a seed of hope (not of despair) into the heart of the counselee. It is not the pastoral counselor's duty to merely make the sheep recover from injuries, but to successfully move them back into society where the victory must be won.

Those women seeking external beauty should be counseled in the biblical words written by Solomon: "Charm is deceptive, and beauty is fleeting; but a woman who fears the Lord is to be praised" (Prov. 31:30, NIV). Possessing the fear of God (Ps. 34:9, 72:5; Eccl. 12:13; Rom. 11:20) is vital for a productive Christian lifestyle. Walking uprightly implies walking in the fear of the Lord. To revere God and His creation is vital for victorious Christian living. Therefore pastoral counselors have the goal to bring counselees into an acceptance of physical shortcomings so that effective ministry can take place in the soul.

CHAPTER 4

CONTROL

O ne day I was helping a friend move into her new home.
She said, "Dawn, you are so anal!" I was being very
precise and placing boxes and containers in the trunk of her
car as if I was putting together a puzzle. After thinking for a
moment, I smiled and said, "There is a good reason for that.
Do you want to hear a good testimony?" I proceeded to tell
her how I was born with many congenital defects, one of
them being an anal fistula. However, the doctors could not
operate for twelve months, and so during that first year of my
life, several enemas had to be administered to me. Because
of my anal problem, I could have become "anal-retentive"
— resistant to change due to the need to control something
that is out of control. The problem with people who have
control issues, though, is that they do not *want* to change.

People must be taught to "let go." Bethany Christian
Services produced a video entitled *Letting Go*. The video
displays life situations and the grief that is felt by a new
mother when placing her baby for adoption. The correct
perspective of control is to be like that baby placed in the
care of another family. When one yields himself to God, He
is in control and not the person.

In the culture where my husband and I were missionaries, I had an opportunity to work for the prefecture government treating psychiatric patients. One man in his late
thirties still lived with his controlling mother. She did every

Rules often
Change
manipulation

domestic chore for him to the point that she even watched over him while taking a bath. This man had never held a job, and wanted to work and help in the house, but he was never given the opportunity. When he came into my office, after asking the traditional professional questions, I began to read the Bible to him. I continued doing so in the following sessions, and eventually he accepted Christ as his personal Savior. His life changed dramatically.

Those who have left "Christian cults" such as Christian Science, Mormonism, and Jehovah's Witness must go through cognitive deprogramming and (often) spiritual deliverance in order to experience true freedom from control. In these institutions, the leaders psychologically manipulate members. Members are told what they can and cannot do. Rules and regulations often change. The key element in these cults is the "spirit of control." Even in legitimate churches, leadership often manifests control. Furthermore there are many marriages in which one of the spouses is controlling. The evil spirit behind this control is subtle (Gen. 2:9, 3:5,22; Ps. 34:21, 119:115; Eccl. 9:3; Is. 1:1-4; Matt. 9:1-4; John 3:1-21; Acts 7:1-6; Rom. 7:19, 12:9).

One man had been clinically depressed for over sixteen years, in and out of hospitals, and on different kinds of medication. His wife was a controlling and angry woman, and she played the role of "mother" in his life, disarming him of his own ability to make decisions. After two weeks of meeting with him, the Lord gave to me the phrase, "Feed my sheep." Jesus was asking me to disciple the counselee. The counselee needed discipleship, memorization of Scripture, and personal teaching on how the Bible could be applied to his past, present, and future life. The problem came when the controlling wife saw that my ministry was edifying him. I became a threat to her because my approach was working and hers was not. Unfortunately a willing man to disciple him could not be found within my local church body, and eventually the wife terminated the sessions with a biblical "excuse." After the counseling sessions ended, intercessory prayer became the only means by which I could minister to them. Then, a few months later, the wife came to me and thanked me! She had begun to forgive those who had hurt her in the past and "give up" the control.

In reality, every human being has encountered situations that have presented the choice to control or not to control. It could be the mother of a teenager, a toddler in potty training, a spouse of a chemically dependent person, or the CEO of a corporation.

One such man had a wife who was a heroin and PCP addict. They had three children. The husband and wife had received the saving grace of Jesus shortly after marriage. However, after the birth of their last child, the wife returned to the pleasures of this world. Through this her husband's faith increased, and he eventually became the caregiver, financial provider, spiritual leader, domestic engineer, and father of his home. The three children were under my care and counsel during the time their father attended Overcomers Anonymous meetings. Five years from the onset, the husband was able to join an early Morning Prayer group. The key element in this prayer time for him was "Thy kingdom come, Thy will be done." Even though he wanted his wife to be emotionally and chemically healed, he yielded the control to God.

CHAPTER 5

DELIVERANCE

Deliverance in the Christian realm can best be described as freedom from demonization. Demonization is the outward or inward influence of a demon upon an individual, who may or may not confess Christ as Savior.

There would be no need for deliverance *unless* people could be demonized. The study of demons (demonology) can be considered from as far back as Adam and Eve. The spirit of deception was working in Eve's life. Then one of her offspring was strongly influenced or demonized, causing him to murder his own brother.

The spiritual gift of discernment of spirits is very useful in deliverance (see 1 Cor. 12:10). As we minister to those who need healing, we must be very discerning in order to pray effectively for release and restoration.[8] Yet *natural* discernment is also valuable and can be learned.

For me personally, this development of natural discernment occurred through answering phones on a crisis hotline for five years in Orange County, California. During that time, I learned to discern, through content and tone of voice, the real versus the unreal urgency of an individual, the sincerity of the heart, and the depth of the person's walk with the Lord.

I furthered developed my natural discernment during four years of missionary work in the Far East. While there, I recognized the effects on the family unit of long past feudal wars and national isolation. There was much physical,

further

31

sexual, and emotional abuse among the people, who gener-
ally had no one trustworthy to talk with about their abuse.
I also discovered that living on an island could increase
feelings of isolation and thus create a heightened source of
nuclear family conflict. *Natural* factors such as these are to
be considered in developing natural discernment.

The most equipped Christian for exercising demons is
not only one who has studied demonology but also more
importantly one who quietly knows the authority he/she has
in the name and the blood of Jesus. It is vital that one has a
clear understanding both of his/her authority over the devil
and the fact that this is a ministry of reconciliation of bound
souls to freedom in Christ. The ministry of deliverance is
seeking to establish or to reestablish an unhindered relationship between God and an individual who is being hindered
by a demonic presence.

The ministry of deliverance cannot be taken lightly.
Demons are real. During my ministry overseas, I saw the
effect of the demonic on souls. Sometimes you must endure
much fasting and prayer to drive these out (see Is. 58:6). I
have seen the results that a lifestyle of fasting and prayer has
in deliverance of those over whom the prayers were made.
They received a true hunger for the Word of God in their lives
and began to obey Him. Therefore personal, private prayer is
an important factor in facilitating freedom for the captives.
Without it, a pastoral counselor is somewhat handicapped.

Daimoniodes, or demon-like, is mentioned in James
3:15, referring to earthly wisdom. When ministering deliverance, one must not rely on earthly wisdom because one
is wrestling with spiritual powers. We can extend this, and
say then that pastoral counselors must not be dependent on
the wisdom of the world. Psychology may have some good
ideas about human personality, but it has no lasting power.

First Corinthians 3:19 tells us, "For the wisdom of this world is foolishness with God" (KJV).

The work of deliverance is a process and must be followed through to completion. There usually are no "quick fixes." It must be the decision of the individual to *desire* deliverance because, after deliverance, the mind needs to be taught to memorize and meditate on Holy Scripture in place of worldly material (see Rom. 12:2a; 2 Tim. 3:16); the will needs to be continually desiring the Lord's will to be done (see Rom. 12:2b; Luke 11:2); and the emotions need to be felt without dominating or ruling (see John 11:35; Rev. 5:4).

Once true deliverance has occurred, self is put in its proper balance. This allows the Holy Spirit to work freely in the believer. Humility is a key attitude to maintain in order to remain delivered; one must continually be filled with positive influences, especially after demons are exorcized. True humility... brings about agreement and harmony between individuals, with understanding, in a peaceful mind, free from fears and agitating passions and moral conflict.[9]

Recovery time for counselees will depend on them. How determined are they to be whole? The healing process will be quicker for someone with a concrete goal to attain.

Finally, in praying for deliverance, one must consider Proverbs 3:5-7a: "Lean on, trust and be confident in the Lord with all your heart and mind, and do not rely on your own insight or understanding. In all your ways know, recognize and acknowledge Him, and He will direct and make straight and plain your paths. Be not wise in your own eyes" (AMP).

CHAPTER 6

EDIBLE IDOLS

Have you found honey? Eat only what you need,
lest you have it in excess and vomit it (Prov. 25:16,
NAS).

W hen one thinks of idolatry, one usually thinks of
paganism and other world religions. However some
of the greatest "idols" in society today could include certain
foods, such as caffeinated drinks, chocolates, and fast food.
An edible idol is something that is consumable by the
human body on a regular, consistent basis, yet does not truly
benefit the body. It is consumed either impulsively or by
habit, and can be harmful to the person.

Eating disorders are a problem in society, including
obesity, bulimia, and anorexia. An obese person is one who
is overweight by 20 percent of his or her combined height
and body frame as a result of overeating (ex. not because
of thyroid problems, medication, etc.). Normally a five-foot,
five-inch woman would ideally weigh no more than 125
pounds. If she weighs 185 pounds or more, she would be
obese by the Body Mass Index. According to the American
Psychiatric Association, bulimia nervosa is a disorder that is
characterized by extreme binge eating at least twice a week
for at least three months in a row. Using a variety of methods,
the individual forces the food to be eliminated out of the
body. An anorexic person is one obsessed with his or her

outward appearance and acceptance from others. Anorexics view food as an enemy because they do not want to gain *any* weight. They are medically diagnosed with this obsession when their body weight is 15% below the average when considering height and body frame.

> Some infants spit up everything; some teenagers will not eat anything. The mothers of babies who ruminate are almost invariably immature and dependent. They are incapable of providing warm, comfortable and intimate physical care for their babies. Often they are severely depressed and spend little time caring for the infant. It sometimes happens that a physician has patients (they are more apt to be women) whose appearances are truly shocking. Their eyes are brilliant. Their cheeks are hollow, and their cheekbones seem to protrude through the skin.[10]

"What agreement is there between the temple of God and idols? For you are the temple of the living God. As God has said: 'I will live with them and walk among them, and I will be their God, and they will be my people'" (2 Cor. 6:16, NIV). Romans 12:1 instructs us to present our *bodies* as holy and living sacrifices to the Lord, which is our reasonable service of worship. Hard core choices must be made (see Deut. 30:19-20).

All kinds of eating problems can be overcome through the fruit of the Holy Spirit such as joy and self-control (Gal. 5:22-23). It would be a misnomer to say that one permanently either can lift oneself up or have control over oneself without God (see John 5:30; 1 Cor. 4:3). We desperately need the empowerment of the Holy Spirit to accomplish this, which is why joy and self-control are products of the Holy Spirit and not the fruit of human endeavors.

Since the state of being downcast is the root of most eating problems, one remedy is for the person to develop joy in his/her life. The Bible reveals that a merry heart is like a medicine (see Prov. 17:22). It also says that a good report makes the bones fat.

Regarding self-control, Proverbs 25:28 says, "He who has no rule over his own spirit is like a city that is broken down and without walls" (AMP).

Trust is the main ingredient in letting go of personal control. One must trust Jesus concerning eternity, but one also must trust Him with one's mind, will, and emotions in this earthly life. One goal for a person with an eating problem is developing an attitude of gratefulness for the way he or she was created. In order to do this, one must change one's concept of God. Many today are denying themselves the privilege of inner transformation and growth because of their inability to reconcile adverse circumstances to their concept of God and His presence.[11]

Those who have been through sexual abuse, for example, have an extremely difficult time relating to a sovereign, all-loving, all-knowing God. Frequently they also have anorexia or bulimia. They will say, "If God is so loving, why didn't He protect me from this?" and, "If He knows everything, why did He knowingly make me go through this?" It is in these situations of despair that the pastoral counselor should systematically teach the life, death, and resurrection of Christ, with an emphasis on the detailed process of a Roman crucifixion. The Roman crucifix is a word picture for those who have been abused. For homework, require the counselee to memorize Hebrews 4:15.

The word "touched" (KJV) in the above-mentioned verse means to commiserate. Jesus sympathizes with every deep pain and has pity. Yet in His presence is fullness of joy, and at His right hand are pleasures forever (Ps. 16:11). He

Jesus has come to exchange sadness and mourning for joy (experience Is. 51:11).

These precious counselees need to be soaked in prayer and in the Word of God. Jesus said that His food was to do the will of the Heavenly Father (see John 4:34). God's sheep in the pastoral counselor's care need to feed on His will, which is found in His Word. They must not perish (physically or spiritually) due to a lack of knowledge of the love letters and promises written in the Bible (see Hos. 4:6; 2 Pet. 1:3-4; Is. 5:13).

Take people with eating problems under your wing and see Jesus transform them. I ministered to a twenty-two year-old woman who had been through three long-term hospitalizations since the age of thirteen. She was addicted to diet drinks and nicotine, and she was tormented by her abusive past. When she came to me for counseling, she did not know if Truth was psychological jargon or the Word of God. I discerned that she needed education both in the Bible and in God as her Father, as well as a nurturing discipleship program. Weeks went by. She became delivered of her haunting past; she began quoting Scripture in the home; and she desired to treat her body like the temple of the living God instead of like an abused piece of trash.

Food is a nourishing substance. Yet the Holy Spirit is our Comforter and Consoler (see John 14:16,26, 15:26, 16:7), not food. Let us teach others to use food accordingly.

"Finally, beloved, keep yourselves from idols" (see 1 John 5:21).

CHAPTER 7

FREEDOM

It is for freedom that Christ has set us free... (Gal. 5:1, NIV).

Freedom is not where you are, but who you are in Christ. As we experience freedom from the repercussions of sin, the turbulence, guilt, and remorse, we gain total liberty to express the fruit of our new nature.[12] Through receiving the Holy Spirit and the resulting character-developing process, our psychological and emotional responses to the sins and traumas of the past are healed.

One little girl and her brother experienced freedom from just talking about the molestation the girl had experienced while her ten year-old brother watched. A family who were foreign missionaries in the same geographical location as me was evangelizing the perpetrators. When I met with the parents, they were concerned about their son's excessive talking and habitual lying, which had begun after the incident. The cause was the boy had not been given an opportunity to vent his emotions of helplessness in the face of two grown men threatening him not to tell anyone while he stood there watching his sister being violated. After I met with the entire family, they all had a sense of relief and freedom from this terrifying experience. Through follow-up calls each month, I received word that the son was functioning like an average boy for his respective developmental stage. He was talking slower, and was increasingly telling the truth. He received emotional freedom that improved his interrelational problems and communication skills.

As one learns how to maintain the mind of Christ, one is emotionally free, no matter what may arise. This is true for persecuted Christians around the world. Richard Wurmbrand was imprisoned for fourteen years for standing for the truth. Mr. Wurmbrand did not lose peace, joy, or love in his life, yet his body sustained many horrific injuries. Christians in China are often subjected to various inhumane acts of torture, and occasionally experience martyrdom.

Again, freedom is not *where* you are, but *who* you are in Christ. One abused wife I counseled had a son who was unjustly sent to prison. While incarcerated, he invited Christ into his heart, and in turn forgave those who had offended him. However, his father harbored unforgiveness towards his family of origin and transferred that anger to his wife. The result was that the son was freer than his father, in spite of his physical imprisonment.

Paul said to the Galatians, "You, my brothers, were called to be free. But do not use your freedom to indulge the sinful nature; rather, serve one another in love. The entire law is summed up in a single command: 'Love your neighbor as yourself'" (5:13-14, NIV). Freedom requires a responsible executor of those freedoms. Only people in bondage abuse or misuse people and their God-given liberty.

Many men who abuse their wives need to be admonished to love their own bodies and to thank God for the way they have been made. They must be free to accept themselves as they physically are (see Eph. 5:28-29). One man I worked with in marriage counseling overcame his abusive tendencies because his wife learned how to appreciate the appearance of his genitals.

If his mother or father sexually shames a man in early childhood or adolescence, the wife can prophetically pronounce healing in his emotions and body (secretly to an unbelieving husband, quietly with a believing one). She can actually be a healing tool in the hands of God for her husband.

Confession of sin results in freedom. The Bible says to "confess your sins to each other and pray for each other so that you may be healed. The prayer of a righteous man is powerful and effective" (James 5:16). In ministry to a woman caught in sexual sin, one pastoral counselor noticed that guilt would trigger fear in her, but "as confession was made, the guilt was removed and the fear dissipated, resulting in perfect freedom."[13]

Many counselors (secular and Christian) have recommended divorce for couples for the purpose of liberation or freedom. However this does not lead to true freedom. Just like cigarettes, drinking, and promiscuity, divorce is often an illogical form of escape from a relational problem. When the Bible says that God gives a way of escape (see 1 Cor. 10:13), it is to escape temptation, not people. The fight is not against people but against demonic forces (see Eph. 6:12), as well as our *own* evil desires (see James 1:14). Essentially, there is no other way to freedom but to trust and obey. This obedience may include pain or suffering, but it is more blessed (see 1 Sam. 15:22).

In regard to freedom, the pastoral counselor must emphasize holy living as opposed to religious living to the counselee. Holy living is a God-given desire to do His will; religious living is done out of obligation or compulsion. Second Corinthians 9:7 exhorts us to do all things cheerfully: "Each man should give what he has decided in his heart to give, not reluctantly or under compulsion, for God loves a cheerful giver" (NIV). This portion of Scripture is textually referring to tangible assets; however God also wants us to *serve* Him with gladness, with a free spirit.

This means that one must do all things heartily as unto the Lord and not for man's approval. True freedom is knowing that the Lord Himself is one's inheritance (see Num. 18:20b; Deut. 18:2b; Josh. 13:33; Ezek. 44:28b). May pastoral counselors radiate this truth and freedom through their lives to all their counselees.

CHAPTER 8

FORGIVENESS

Immediately following His teaching on prayer, Jesus said, "For if you forgive people their trespasses — that is, their reckless and willful sins, leaving them, letting them go and giving up resentment — your heavenly Father will also forgive you" (Matt. 6:14, AMP). Then He declared, "If you do not forgive others their trespasses — their reckless and willful sins, leaving them, letting them go and giving up resentment — neither will your Father forgive you your trespasses" (Matt. 6:15, AMP).

Many have asked, "What is true forgiveness?" and "How do I know I have forgiven someone?" The answer is in the heart. No pastor, therapist, or counselor can truly answer that question. However there are times during a counseling session when the Lord divinely reveals to a counselor the state of the counselee's heart, but this is always for the purpose of further healing, never for judgment. Romans 2:1-4 speaks against judgment, for it is God's judgment and His kindness that leads us to repentance.

In my own life I have found the Lord's divine kindness to be true. When I became a Christian, I despised my parents for not teaching me the biblical way to salvation. I opened the door for unforgiveness, and thereby developed an inward rebellion toward my parents. Then one day while reading the Bible, the Holy Spirit revealed to me that I needed to ask for a supernatural love for my parents — not a feeling, but an act of my will. I decided to love them, and by His grace I put on love according to Colossians 3:13.

I did not have any right to place myself in the position of God, deciding how He should ordain my steps by telling Him what kind of family in which I should have been reared. Fortunately, as a pre-teen, the Lord was able to work with my heart in a quick manner. Yet this is often not so as people get older and more settled in their ways. The Bible calls this being "stiff-necked."

Stiff-necked means obstinate or stubborn, coming from the Hebrew word *qasheh*. It also means to be dense or tough, from the Hebrew word *qashah*. The Lord commands us to circumcise our hearts and stop being stiff-necked (practice Deut. 10:16). Stephen corrected his persecutors, saying, "You stiff-necked people, with uncircumcised hearts and ears! You are just like your fathers: You always resist the Holy Spirit" (Acts 7:51, NIV). Upon hearing the convicting words, the council stoned him. Experience agrees with this, in that over the years I have found that most people living in unforgiveness are resistant to the work of the Holy Spirit and the words of His ministers.

I have found that the manner of correction is a key. One must give correction in a loving manner. Tone of voice has almost everything to do with it. The majority of the communication and its effectiveness are determined by how calm, cool, and collected one is when giving and receiving corrective words. "A soft answer turneth away wrath: but grievous words stir up anger" (Prov. 15:1, KJV). "He that is slow to anger is better than the mighty; and he that ruleth his spirit than he that taketh a city" (Prov. 16:32, KJV).

I had been successfully counseling a teen and her single mother through some difficult interpersonal problems. After some months, the girl's boyfriend wanted to receive biblical counsel. Then I found out about his mother, who had been married seven times and was a senior pastor of a small church.

She had been trying to counsel her son about marriage. I became almost indignant, and went to his mother. I used a question and answer form of dialogue and a low, calm tone of voice. "Have you been married seven times?" was one of my first questions to clarify matters (not "I hear you have been married seven times"). Then afterwards I said to her, "Now your son is very confused about the characteristics of a godly relationship." I admit I had no authority in that woman's life because she had not given it to me. I attempted an intervention, but it was unsuccessful; the pastoral counseling process ended for all concerned. I had to repent before the Lord and forgive myself for being so unwise.

"You're grounded", or "You can't go to the game", or some other kind of punishment is often given to our children as they grow up. In turn, they usually respond with, "I'm sorry", and they are sorry, but usually sorry they were caught doing something wrong. Ordinarily they are not repentant, but are attempting to change the parent's mind. For this reason, I teach children to re-word their apologies. "Will you forgive me for pulling the baby's hair?" or "Would you forgive me for going on the Internet without your permission?" I also teach parents to provoke their children to think about the consequences of their behavior and later express forgiveness after careful discussion has been made. At the end of the discussion, the child is telling the parent why his/her behavior was wrong. As a result, in the future the compliant child will think twice before committing such behavior because of this humble, responsible, and repentant process. At the same time, parents must remember that it is vital, when moral behavior is at stake, that they do not change their minds regarding correction. The principle of repentance and forgiveness is difficult when there is no set standard in the home — that is, a criterion for the basis of making a judgment.

Forgiveness is a foundational principle of Christianity *because* there are rules not to be broken. However secular humanism and most psychological theories do not promote the ministry of forgiveness because according to them, rules are *relative*. If it *feels* right, do it, they say. Yet you cannot respond to situations based on impulse or emotions. Forgiveness is a decision that must be made using the will. Luke 6:36-37 uses the imperative voice, "Be merciful, just as your Father is merciful. And do not judge, and you will not be judged; and do not condemn, and you will not be condemned; pardon, and you will be pardoned" (NAS).

The significant aspect about the woman caught in the act of adultery is not the fact that Jesus wrote in the sand, nor did it matter with whom she transgressed. It was the act of forgiveness ministered by Jesus. Pastoral counselors must be the (prophetic) ministers of the Lord (1 Cor. 4:1; 2 Cor. 3:6, 6:3-11). They must minister the truth in love, and not become like the Pharisees who wanted to stone her. Christ's love must shine through them by effectively listening to the counselee's real *or* imaginary pain, looking the counselee intently in the eyes, occasionally leaning forward to show interest in the person, and at times repeating things spoken to keep the counselee mindful of effective communication.

Forgiveness always requires effective communication. Speaking is not always enough. Forgiving communication is also shown through our actions and body language. People must be made mindful of this.

Furthermore, forgiveness is a conditional act. *If* you forgive, *then* you are forgiven (Eph. 4:32). Conditional forgiveness is mentioned at least seven times in the New Testament and eighteen times in the Old Testament. The original word in Hebrew, *calach*, means forgive, pardon, or spare. A classic Old Testament verse that clearly explains this type of forgiveness is Second Chronicles 7:14, "If my people who are called by my name shall humble themselves, pray, seek, crave and require of necessity My face, and turn from their wicked ways, then will I hear from Heaven, forgive their sin, and heal their land" (AMP). Luke 6:37-38 are also conditional verses: "Judge not, and ye shall not be judged: condemn not, and ye shall not be condemned: forgive, and ye shall be forgiven: Give and it shall be given unto you; good measure, pressed down, and shaken together, and running over, shall men give into your bosom. For with the same measure that ye mete withal it shall be measured to you again" (KJV).

The result of unforgiveness is bitterness. Unforgiveness produces bitter poison that defiles many. Our society has been overly encouraged to "vent one's feelings" by main-stream psychology. Secular and Christian clients have been trained to dwell on and express true feelings at all times inadvertently producing selfish attitudes and evading personal responsibility for sin. Yet dwelling on hurt or pain produces self-pity, mourning, or bitterness. Dwelling is a form of worship because it involves concentration on an object, as does worship. The Bible says that he who dwells (settles) in the secret place of the Most High shall abide under the shadow of the Almighty (see Ps. 91:1). Pastoral counselors must train their counselees to settle in on the Lord rather than the pain, anger, hurt, or disappointment.

Unforgiveness, if not resolved, becomes a stronghold. A stronghold is translated as "strength" twenty times in the Old Testament. In Hebrew, it means stronghold, force, or fortress. "A brother offended is harder to be won than a strong city, and contentions are like the bars of a castle" (Prov. 18:19, NAS). Unforgiveness keeps people in bondage. It keeps them from advancing in the kingdom of God. This means forgiveness is not only an emotional process but also a spiritual decision.

Finding a resolution must be the goal for the pastoral counselor in helping someone suffering from unforgiveness. Exhort them to choose life by forgetting what lies behind (see Phil. 3:13; James 1:23-24). Help them through the process of forgiveness.

The focus of repentance must be greater than that of others' offenses (see Matt. 7:1-5). Help counselees to pray by leading them in a prayer of repentance each time they come until they don't want to talk about offenses any more. And remember: just to say "I'm sorry" is not enough. True repentance incorporates the words, "Will you forgive me for _____?" which involves an attitude and act of humility. God resists the proud, but gives grace to the humble (see Ps. 138:6; Matt. 23:12; James 4:6).

CHAPTER 9

GERONTOLOGY

...But [as for] you, teach what is fitting and becoming to sound doctrine — the character and right living that identify true Christians. Urge the older men to be temperate, venerable (serious), sensible, self-controlled; sound in the faith, in the love, and in the steadfastness and patience [of Christ]. Bid the older women similarly to be reverent and devout in their deportment, as becomes those engaged in sacred service, not slanderers or slaves to drink. They are to give good counsel and be teachers of what is right and noble, so they will wisely train the young women to be sane and sober-minded — temperate, disciplined — and to love their husbands and their children; to be chaste, homemakers, good-natured (kindhearted), adapting and subordinating themselves to their husbands, that the word of God may not be exposed to reproach — blasphemed or discredited (Titus 2:1-5, AMP).

Out of all the passages in the Bible, this one seems to be the ultimate purpose for aging people. Surprisingly, it also seems to be what the study of geriatrics has taught behavioral scientists. Eric Erikson is the behavioral scientist that was noted for his documentation on the stages of life. He calls the last stage generativity versus stagnation. Erikson supports the idea that people in the golden years will either use their gifts and talents to benefit society or will stagnate into the melting pot of retired citizens who see little to no purpose for their lives.

Today it is the "baby boomers" who are also the "sand-wich generation" — the forty and above year-olds who are in the position of deciding on the domestic destiny of their aging parent(s). Home care, hospice care, nursing homes, or their own home, depending on the situation and the community in which they live, give the boomers a variety of choices.

Throughout the centuries and leading up to WWII, aging parents stayed in the home until death. In most countries around the world, this is still the case. In the Asian nation where my husband and I were missionaries, there is this healthy system for the golden year population. Due to the small land mass and the Buddhist and Confucianist religious practices, the aged are a value to society. They keep the household farm growing, the grandchildren occupied, and fresh food present on the family altar morning by morning. Few are left without a purpose in life. Few become seriously ill since they are also active.

Yet as western society becomes busier and more modern-ized and the Bible increasingly is removed from society, hope for the aged dwindles. One answer is to encourage teenagers to find a golden year Christian who has stayed with the Lord for a long time in order to listen to all the wonderful things Christ has done in his or her life. This will accomplish at least three benefits: 1) the teen will hear the benefits of commitment and faithfulness to the Lord, 2) the golden year believer will sense that they have sown good seed into a young person's life, and 3) both parties will be in an attitude of gratitude (see Col. 3:17; 1 Thess. 5:18).

Ministering to those who are physically dying does not involve formal discipleship from a manual; rather the ministry of discipleship can be in teaching them how to die without fear. The Lord might lead the pastoral counselor by His Spirit to sing a hymn or a worship song with him or her. The patient may also be comforted by a special Bible passage. The pastoral counselor can build another's faith by reading or praying the Word of God (see Rom. 10:17), such as, "Thank you, Lord, that precious is the death of your loved ones in your sight, and that You have given my beloved brother (or sister) the victory that has overcome the world, even his (or her) faith" (see Ps.116:15; 1 John 5:4).

Soap operas, which are viewed by many aging Americans, especially in nursing homes and public institutions, facilitate an attitude of monotony, boredom, and hopelessness. Jesus works against these by giving us creativity and hope to live life abundantly (see John 10:10; Rom. 8:24-25). The pastoral counselor must be creative in helping those in their golden years redeem the time. Redeeming the time... is to regain, through the redemptive power of the cross, lost opportunities. Each one of our lives is an epistle, known and read of all men. Through the redemptive power of Christ, expedited through forgiveness, let us rewrite the pages of our life history where we have sinned or responded negatively to the reproofs of life.[14]

God has given biological and surrogate Christian grandparents from whom younger people can learn and glean. We should seize the day while we still call it day (see Heb. 3:12-4:1) to be exhorted by those who have an interest in our spiritual well being. Let us exhort the younger ones to care for the elderly in the church. Those in the golden years of life have volumes of history to pass on to the next generation. If this loving action is expressed seriously and sincerely, it could be life changing.

If a golden-ager has Alzheimer's disease, one may want to take steps in learning all one can about the illness. We do not have to look far into the church community to find those suffering from Alzheimer's disease. Practical family support is necessary when a loved one is in the late stages of this illness — memory loss, hiding things, wandering off like a lost child. If the husband is afflicted, the elderly wife is often too weak to care for such a person. We can encourage youth or college age groups to rotate with the care of these individuals.

One woman who was in a large denominational church received little help when her husband became advanced in Alzheimer's disease. When they finally stopped going to church, only one church member called. Eventually she needed a home care nurse to bathe her husband. The only encouragement she received was from her immediate family and from Christian television.

Many emotional healings could have been accomplished in her life had the church cared. Someone could have called once a week just to encourage the future widow by listening to her struggles. Someone occasionally could have either visited her with a care basket of fruit or sent a bouquet of flowers for her birthday. "So then, as occasion and opportunity are open to us, let us do good (morally) to all people [not only being useful or profitable to them, but also doing what is for their spiritual good and advantage]. Be mindful to be a blessing, especially to those of the household of faith — those who belong to God's family with you, the believers" (Gal. 6:10, AMP).

The Bible says that pure and undefiled religion in the sight of our Father is to visit orphans and widows in their distress, and to keep oneself unstained by the world (James 1:27). A widow is someone whose husband has died. A widow indeed is one without husband or children (1 Tim. 5:4). The widows indeed must be honored and respected while the younger ones should be encouraged to remarry (1 Tim. 5:3,11). An immediate remarriage (on the rebound) due to loneliness, however, is not recommended. Many widows and widowers who have started dating within six months of their loss have emotionally damaged the life of the new spouse or the lives of any children involved. Rather an emotional inventory needs to be taken by the widow or widower in order for a healthy transition to take place. This is practical advice that I have discussed in the next chapter on grief.

Companionship is a major reason that the elderly remarry, according to authorities on gerontology. Ruth saw this need in Naomi and became her companion for life (see Ruth 1:16). Loneliness is a common disposition of many people today, and our aging population is usually the hardest hit by this. It is entirely possible that many of our dearly beloved silver saints will die because loneliness has set in.

Pastoral counselors must always be considerate of the needs of others, especially those whom society takes advantage of — the disabled, mentally ill, and elderly. Listen to a part of the letter of Paul to the Romans:

Do not be conformed to this world — this age, fashioned after and adapted to its external, superficial customs. But be transformed (changed) by the |entire| renewal of your mind — by its new ideals and its new attitude — so that you may prove [for yourselves] what is the good and acceptable and perfect will of God, *even* the thing which is good and acceptable and perfect |in His sight for you|. For by the grace (unmerited favor of God) given to me I warn every one among you not to estimate *and* think of himself more highly than he ought — not to have an exaggerated opinion of his own importance; but to rate his ability with sober judgment, each according to the degree of faith apportioned by God to him. So we, numerous as we are, are one body in Christ, the Messiah, and individually we are parts one of another — mutually dependent on one another (Rom. 12:2-3,5 AMP, emphasis added).

CHAPTER 10

GRIEF

Emotions are a natural part of life. We cannot ignore them. Some secular *and* Christian therapists have focused on the emotion of the counselee to the point that an attitude of selfishness and "victimization" has developed in many who go to these professionals. Yet pastoral counselors must help counselees to recognize that "worldly" grief (see 2 Cor. 7:10) — vacillating among anger, denial, bargaining, depression, and acceptance — is not the key to healing. The answer to grief is godly sorrow that facilitates true repentance.

Judas Iscariot gave into the temptation to betray Christ. Instead of godly sorrow, however, he had deep remorse (*metamellomai*), which in turn led to extreme guilt, because he did not take responsibility for his lack of character.

Ahithophel saw that his advice was not followed, and like Judas, went and hanged himself (see 2 Sam. 17:23). An interesting point is that he put his house in order before committing suicide. Pastoral counselors can identify false repentance by religious acts that follow without character or heart change.

True repentance calls for the reception of God's forgiveness and a turning away from the sin that so easily entangles. The heart of repentance is returning to the starting point — Jesus, our first love.

This is the same principle that I often use in pre-marital and marital counseling. If one spouse says to another that they have lost their love in marriage, I ask them to reminisce about their engagement period or about what he or she was attracted to in the other's character. Be aware though that pastoral counselors should be careful when asking these questions about marriages in which neither partner is saved.

During times of grief, it is very common for issues of the past to rise to the surface. I ministered to earthquake survivors who experienced the Kobe, Japan earthquake of 1995, in which almost five thousand lives were lost. Many of the ones I counseled were more than sixty-five years of age. I counseled these unsaved loved ones of Jesus by listening to them according to James 1:19. I discovered that the elderly also wanted to grieve over the losses of World War II. They told stories of radiation problems caused by the atomic bombs, of loss of parents, of famine in the land, and of literal dependence on others for survival. I remember the Holy Spirit speaking to me and saying, "It is not time to share the gospel with words, because you are showing My love by your action of listening." Pastoral counseling does not always incorporate the spoken word. God often will reveal knowledge or wisdom for the purpose of effective prayer and intercession on another's behalf rather than for verbalizing.

After the loss of a ministry position (by termination or choice), there are many temptations that Satan may throw at us. For some, the ministry can be addicting. I, for one, came to experience hundreds of calls a week from people requesting prayer by the time I was only twenty-three years old! By choice I resigned, married, and served as a foreign missionary for four years. One might say that as I entered the foreign mission field, I was on the rebound to ministry. That would have been the case if the place we served was "ripe unto harvest", but it was not. I suffered through withdrawals and mourning by murmuring and complaining for two years until I could finally socialize with the native people. What I did not realize until much later was that through the "grieving" of serving in a very difficult foreign ministry, the Lord Himself wanted to woo me into a more intimate relationship with Him. In the end, I experientially discovered both that full-time ministry is not always a position, and that ministry must be secondary to our relationship with Jesus.

Paul infers that love (and God is love) is the answer for those who may be saddened by loss. "For out of much affliction and anguish of heart I wrote to you with many tears; not that you should be made sorrowful, but that you might know the love which I have especially for you" (2 Cor. 2:4, NAS). As pastoral counselors, we must convey this love to our counselees in real and practical ways. I have written letters to my clients at times to emphasize God's love for them. Other times (before scandals were commonplace) I have held female clients to assure them of motherly or sisterly love.

In the spring of 1999, God used the death of a missionary doctor and his two sons in the nation of India to see many Hindus come to Christ. This seemingly unfortunate family event could be summed up in Jesus' following words: "I assure you, most solemnly I tell you, unless a grain of wheat falls into the earth and dies, it remains [just one grain; never becomes more but lives] by itself alone. But if it dies, it produces many others *and* yields a rich harvest. Any one who loves his life loses it. But any one who hates his life in this world will keep it to life eternal. Whoever has no love for, no concern for, no regard for his life here on earth, but despises it, preserves his life forever and ever" (John 12:24-25, AMP, emphasis added).

In my own life, Jesus called me to count the cost when I was asked to be a full-time foreign missionary by my future husband. At the time, I was already in a full-time ministry that I thoroughly enjoyed. However the Lord spoke to my heart as I was seeking direction concerning this decision, saying, "Are you willing to join yourself to this man and his vision so that he can obtain favor from Me?" (see Prov. 18:22). I was called to lay down my ambitions to serve another's vision. I am often reminded of this when I sing the song, "In Thy presence Lord, in Thy presence Lord. I desire to be continually in Thy presence Lord. As I lift my hands before You, I lay down all my ambitions. I just desire to be continually in Thy presence Lord."

Many parents have ambitions and plans for their children, and thus they do not encourage their children to have their own dreams and visions. Parents must let go of their own desires and help their children find the revealed word of the Lord. When they receive this revelation, they need to be encouraged by pondering it in their hearts and laboring in intercession for the vision to come to pass.

Travailing and mourning must always end in praise for healing to take place (see Is. 51:11, 61:1-3; Jer. 31:11-13; Ps. 30:10-31:1). Hannah was in travailing prayer for a child (see 1 Sam. 1:10). She was mourning over the ridicule and disgrace of being barren. Her trial, however, ended in beautiful praise to God and answered prayer (see 1 Sam. 1:19-20, 2:1-10; Ps. 113:1-9). In reality, God does not always work the same way for each woman struck with barrenness as He did for Sarah (Gen. 11:30,18:11, 21:1-2), Rebekah (Gen. 25:19-21), Rachel (Gen. 29:31, 30:1,22-23), Manoah's wife (Judges 13:2-3), and Hannah (1 Sam. 1:5,19-20). Some married women remain physically barren for their entire lives.

One woman I know found out at the age of nineteen, through the means of a routine medical examination, that she could not have children. This particular teen had been praying for a special godly mate from the time she was sixteen. Instead of getting depressed due to the loss of natural motherhood, she began praying specifically for a husband who would faithfully accept her condition. Eight years later, the Lord blessed her with a husband fully devoted to Christ and His ministry. She was never to be a reproach, because a revelatory word came to her during a personal Bible study: "Thou shalt no longer be termed Forsaken; neither shall thy land any more be termed Desolate: but thou shalt be called Hephzibah, and thy land Beulah: for the LORD delighteth in thee, and thy land shall be married" (Is. 62:4, KJV). Hephzibah means "my delight is in her", and Beulah means "married", symbolizing her future blessings and prosperity.

I have often told those in various grieving situations, "Rest in the Lord" (see Ps. 37:7, 116:7; Heb. 4:9). The book of Hebrews mentions a rest for God's people. This is important, because the biggest enemy of proper healing of any emotional issue is "busyness." Even being about the Lord's business on behalf of others can prevent one's own healing from taking place. In fact, often God's people and ministers remain busy for God in order to avoid dealing with their own personal problems.

I knew one man who was a pastoral counselor for a local church. Before becoming a Christian, he was an alcoholic and a womanizer. When I met him, he was already on his second marriage. He was a "dry drunk", obsessively-compulsively addicted to the ministry, and was not necessarily "ordained or arranged in an orderly manner" as the Greek meaning implies. He, like many, went into the pastoral counseling ministry without working through some vital issues himself. In particular, he had some unresolved issues regarding rejection from significant others. With this issue being unresolved, he eventually turned to sin by committing adultery during his second marriage and was subsequently removed from the ministry.

Grief and mourning come in many forms and as the result of diverse situations. As pastoral counselors, we are called by the Lord to be sensitive to the Holy Spirit and His words of comfort, correction, and edification (see John 14:16-17, 16:7-11; Rom. 15:1-2). Let us encourage others to go on with life, even as Joseph did.

And when the days of mourning for him were past, Joseph spoke to the household of Pharaoh saying, "If now I have found favor in your sight, please speak to Pharaoh, saying, 'My father made me swear, saying, "Behold, I am about to die; in my grave which I dug for myself in the land of Canaan, there you shall bury me."' Now therefore, please let me go up and bury my father; then I will return" (Gen. 50:4-5, NAS).

CHAPTER 11

HETEROSEXUALITY

King Solomon said to the Shulamite woman, "You are altogether beautiful, my darling, and there is no blemish in you" (Song. 4:7, NAS). One of the most invaluable interpretations of the Song of Solomon is that of a romantic marriage between a husband and wife.

Marriage is slowly becoming an antiquated word in modern, industrial societies. In America, there are "politically correct" and "politically incorrect" words to discredit the mandates of the Bible concerning marriage. Yet the Bible is clear: "Let marriage be held in honor — esteemed worthy, precious, [that is,] of great price and especially dear — in all things. And thus let the marriage bed be (kept honored) undefiled; for God will judge *and* punish the unchaste (all guilty of sexual vice) and adulterous" (Heb. 13:4, AMP, emphasis added). The word "undefiled" is *amiantos* in Greek, which means pure. The opposite of the word undefiled is defiled. Defiled is *miaino* in Greek, meaning contaminated.

There is a battle between purity and contamination when it comes to human sexuality. Fornication, mentioned thirty-six times in the Bible, is rooted in mental contamination. Thirty-two of the references refer to the Greek word *porneuo* or *porneia*, from which we get the English words pornography and pornographic. The *logos* word of God exhorts His children: "The night is nearly over, the day is almost here. Let us behave decently, as in the daytime, not in orgies and drunkenness, not in sexual immorality and debauchery, not in dissension and jealousy. Rather, clothe yourselves with the Lord Jesus Christ, and do not think about how to gratify the desires of the sinful nature" (Rom. 13:12-13, NIV). We must think on things that are lovely (acceptable), of a good report, and virtuous.

Sex is lovely activity. Sexual intercourse was intended for a husband and wife both to procreate and to express emotional bonding to one another. *Intended for Pleasure*, written by Dr. Ed Wheat, M.D., is an excellent book, and is recommended for marital and engaged pre-marital couples to help them understand the purpose of foreplay and inter-course within the marital union.

During the course of pre-marital counseling for (hetero-sexual) couples, the Lord regularly directs me to minister accountability. The Holy Spirit will periodically have me ask the man and woman, individually or together, directly and specifically about their level of sexual involvement with each other. He does this for the purpose of keeping them pure before marriage.

The Lord has even revealed to me at times that a couple was involved physically beyond what would be considered safe. During one particular session, the Holy Spirit revealed to me that there was some sexual caressing occurring among a couple. The woman affirmed that this was a fact. That gave me an open door to minister the verse, "For ye are bought with a price: therefore glorify God in your body, and in your spirit, which are God's. Now concerning the things whereof ye wrote unto me: It is good for a man not to touch a woman" (1 Cor. 6:20-7:1, KJV).

Men and women of upper, middle, and lower classes in every nation practice prostitution. Prostitution is not a mere act; it is the fruit of hatred for men. Those who have had intercourse with a prostitute have come into a spiritual bonding with that spirit of murder.[15]

Many men and women who have been molested as children have also come into contact with that spirit of murder and hatred of the opposite gender. One woman confided that she was made to orally copulate a man when she was six years of age. This was an event that had been suppressed for nearly ten years until she had directly asked the Lord, at the age of sixteen, why she was neither interested in young men nor in dating. Then, while in prayer one day, He brought to her remembrance the molestation of ten years prior. He did this so that healing through forgiveness could occur (see 1 John 2:9-10, 3:10-11, 4:7-8).

If we really want the life of Jesus to be manifested in our lives, then we must pattern our lives after the Holy Spirit (see Rom. 8:1-14, 13:14; 1 Cor. 6:15-20; 2 Tim. 2:22). Pastoral counselors must ask their counselees questions such as, "How is your thought life (which is where the works of the flesh begin)?" and "What are the meditations of your heart?" (ask Ps. 19:14, 119:97,99) or "What specific temptations try to overtake you?" (ask 1 Cor. 10:13). A good biblical verse to minister to counselees is the following:

Blessed, happy, to be envied is the man who is patient under trial *and* stands up under temptation, for when he has stood the test *and* been approved he will receive [the victor's] crown of life which God has promised to those who love Him. Let no one say when he is tempted, I am tempted from God; for God is incapable of being tempted by [what is] evil and He Himself tempts no one. But every person is tempted when he is drawn away, enticed *and* baited by his own evil desire (lust, passions). (James 1:12-14, AMP, emphasis added)

When pastoral counselors start asking personal questions by the interview method, they must be aware of their own weakness (Gal. 6:1). Many counselors fall into sin because they are high-minded and fail to pass on cases they know are emotionally too difficult for them. One man in a church pastoral care ministry committed the sin of adultery, possibly because he did not refer this case to a qualified and anointed woman pastoral minister *and* he had not dealt with the sin of his past that kept him in bondage throughout his life of multiple marriages.

Sexual sin can be an individual sin while also being a corporate sin indirectly (as in concupiscence/lust, masturbation, pornography, and moral uncleanness — exegete 1 Cor. 6:18, 10:8; Col. 3:4-7; 1 Thess. 4:7; 1 Tim. 6:9; 1 Pet. 2:11) because it ultimately affects human relationships (in cases of harlotry [including adultery and incest] — see 2 Chron. 21:11; Eph. 5:3; in cases of sodomy — see Deut. 23:17; Rom. 1:22-28; 1 Cor. 6:9; and in cases of licentiousness [which is "outrageous behavior" in Greek] — see Mark 7:18-23; Eph. 4:17-19). *Note: Outrageous behavior can also include what professional therapists refer to in their diagnostic manual as exhibitionism. Many individual children have been "over-sensualized" by seeing parents, older siblings, and other physically matured people nude before an age that was emotionally acceptable for them.*

One 24 year-old man, who was not a Christian, came to be counseled. His presenting problem was that he was not married for fear of intimacy with a woman his age. The client voluntarily revealed that he had seen his parents in sexual activity with his father on top of his mother. This disturbed him greatly because he thought his father was doing something "bad" to his mother. The client also had taken baths with his mother until the age of eight or nine. This had caused an over bonding to the mother and a distance from the father. The act of emotional catharsis seemed to help him during the course of active listening, but personal salvation, forgiveness toward his father, and breaking emotional soul ties with his mother would have been part of my treatment plan for him, had he been willing.

When referring to interpersonal marital/heterosexual problems, it is scriptural (see Prov. 5:18-19; Song 2:5-6, 8:2-3) and helpful to talk about sexual positioning. One woman who was separated from her husband did not want to talk extensively about sexual issues, but the Lord revealed to me through intercession for her that this was the root of some of her marital unhappiness. She had taken the "martyr" or "masochistic" role in the marriage. She was proud of that, which gave place to spiritual pride. The Lord led me to ask her if she had ever taken the upper position in intercourse with her husband. After a long pause she proclaimed, "There are more positions than that!" I simply communicated with her that she was going to have to face her sexual insecurities eventually and that doing so was preferable while married to the husband of her youth.

Heterosexual, marital intercourse is acceptable sexual behavior in the Bible, and it begins with emotional bonding, not infatuation. Many marriages were begun on worldly (fleshly) standards. Either both partners were unsaved, or one or both were Christians yet settled for second-best (see 2 Cor. 6:14-15). Homosexuality, on the other hand, is not acceptable sexual behavior in the Bible because it involves sodomy, effeminateness, moral uncleanness, and outrageous behavior. In ministry to those who have repented from homosexual sin, a prayer of deliverance and breakage of ungodly soul ties must be embraced. A prayer such as, "Heavenly Father, I break and renounce evil spiritual and emotional ties that I have had with _____(name partner). I renounce these evil ties. I ask you to break them, and I proclaim they are washed away by the shed blood of my Savior Jesus Christ."

Many men and women who have been molested as children experience difficulty in their sexual life. The anger that they displace onto their spouse must be redirected into forgiveness for the perpetrator. Ritual abuse survivors must also work through the process of forgiveness even if they cannot remember *each* time they were violated. Jesus said that we must forgive those who have sinned against us (obey Matt. 18:21-22). The point God is making is not to keep a record of wrong (obey 1 Cor. 13:4-7). First Corinthians 13:5, in the King James Version, says that love does not behave unseemly, seeketh not her own, is not easily provoked, and thinketh no evil. The word "thinketh" is *logizomai* in Greek, meaning to take inventory, to reason, to conclude.

Common knowledge among marriage counselors is that the brain is the largest sex organ in the body. This is why affection stimulates the woman to desire her husband and usually allows her to achieve orgasm. "Orgasm" is not specifically mentioned in the Bible, yet one can see an analogy of several sexual responses in Song of Solomon 1:2 and 4:10. These verses are talking about love being better than wine. However the God-given eros love between a husband and wife can also intoxicate. God may want us to *remember* our spouse's love more than wine (remember Song 1:4). Many times I have said to my loving husband, "I remember last night", or "I remember Saturday morning", in response to his love, and as a prelude to the next time we share our love for one another.

Proverb 7:18 can be encouraging to a married, heterosexual couple (although in context it refers to the harlot): "Come, let us drink our fill of love until morning; let us delight ourselves with caresses" (NAS). Caressing is a natural part of love expressed between a husband and wife in a healthy, balanced, interrelationship in which there are no outbursts of wrath, each is easily entreated, and both are trying to be as selfless as possible.

Some television programming, movies, video games, and the Internet have been enemies of intimacy in marriage. At times the Holy Spirit will prompt me to ask a husband or wife about a specific thing, such as the Internet, and exactly about what they are constantly meditating on. Randomly asking verbal questions encourages accountability as mentioned in a previous chapter.

Many marital goals can be accomplished through effective bonding during the first year of marriage by reading Christian marital books together before retiring at night, by writing letters to one another, by sending emails to each other, or by just sitting in the same room together without any interruptive noise or telephones to answer (because the ringer is turned off).

Deuteronomy 24:5 states, "When a man hath taken a new wife, he shall not go out to war, neither shall he be charged with any business: but he shall be free at home one year, and shall cheer up his wife which he hath taken" (KJV). One point here is that adequate rest with one another must be taken to ensure a solid foundation of prayer, financial soundness, and intimacy. Another point is that it is a time for the wife to be cheered up by her husband. The Hebrew word for "cheer up" means to cause to rejoice or be glad. It is in the husband's best interest for the longevity of the marriage to learn everything about his wife as he possibly can about affection and what "turns her on." Likewise, a wife must study her husband and seek the times when he can be uplifted verbally and emotionally (see Song 2:3, 5:16).

A wise pastor once said, "You can make your man feel ten inches tall or ten feet tall by the words of your mouth" (see Prov. 18:21). We have the creative ability to speak edifying words that will foster intimacy, because intimacy and bonding are the goals of heterosexuality. "For this cause a man shall leave his father and his mother, and shall cleave to his wife; and they shall become one flesh, and they were both naked and not ashamed" (Gen. 2:24-25).

CHAPTER 12

HYPERACTIVITY

For many important works of God, there are also counter-feits from Satan. False witnesses (see Ps. 27:12; Matt. 26:59), false prophets (see Matt. 7:15), and false believers (see 2 Cor. 11:26; Gal. 2:4) are among us. The root of false-hood is deception, lying, or jealousy that produces symp-toms of hyperactivity in the form of debate, defensiveness, or rebellion (see Gen. 3:1-6; Acts 5:1-10), fits of rage, irra-tional behavior, manipulation, and suicide (see 1 Sam. 18:7-11,17-29, 19:1,9-10, 20:30-31,33, 22:6-8,13,16-17, 23:8, 24:2, 26:2, 28:3,5,7-8,23, 31:4).

The life of King Saul is one of the longest bibliographies in the Bible (1 Sam. 9:2-31:12), and thus we can obtain much information about his life and his specific behaviors. He was full of fear; he called his own son a bastard; he was obsessed with murder; and he blamed others. The Bible does not mention how Saul was reared. One thing is certain though — he was not medicated. He was not on Ridilin, Dexadrine,  *Ritalin* or Aderall.

Today many children take prescription drugs for what is now known as Attention Deficit Disorder (ADD) and Attention Deficit-Hyperactivity Disorder (ADHD). According to "Children and Adults with Attention Deficit Disorders" (C.H.A.D.D., www.chadd.org), the term ADD was not formally recognized until 1980. The first recogni-tion of children exhibiting inattentiveness, impulsivity, and hyperactivity did not occur until 1902. These children some-times exhibit drastically improved behavior when religiously medicated. Accountability, drug education, and responsi-bility on the part of the caregiver are necessary in this area. Parents must be committed both to prayer and the success of the medical profession. If they are familiar with the different types of related prescription drugs, the parent may assist the physician in his or her own child's healing.

Children like this must be treated both in and out of the church as if he or she was a diabetic or an asthmatic (they all need medication). Other children must be disciplined with different techniques (see Prov. 22:6,15, 23:13 [AMP], 29:15; Luke 2:43-49; Heb. 12:5-11). Some children are mellow and self-disciplined; positive reinforcement will work with them most of the time, along with group discipleship. Others are hyperactive and impulsive; they need random monitoring and one-on-one discipleship.

If left to themselves, most hyperactive children will get nothing productive accomplished. They need directive and encouraging words. The peaceable fruit of righteousness is the result of effective discipline and one-on-one communica-tion with hyperactive children. Chastening, according to the Greek, refers to teaching and instructing. Often these children are taught in a public school setting, but may benefit much better from a home school setting. Home school associations can offer more of a controlled environment for hyperactive and impulsive children with more positive ways to exercise their energy.

The word of God commands us to be at peace with all people as is possible for us (see Rom. 12:18). Blessed are the peacemakers because they will be called the children of God (Matt. 5:9). One of the Holy Spirit's fruits is peace (Gal. 5:22-23). Most hyperactive children and adults are not very good peacemakers, but they can be through the power of the Holy Spirit (see Phil. 2:13). They must apply prayer and willful effort (see Dan. 9:3-4; Phil. 2:12). All things are possible with God.

The logos word of God overrides personality. Our society has believed and relied too much on secular philosophies and doctrines of men. True children of God, whether sanguine or hyperactive (diagnosed or not), will behave like one through the Christian maturation process. Those involved in church leadership are encouraged to examine from Scripture how God accomplishes, achieves and develops our personality, and brings us into a state of manhood. Although there is a "common grace" in which God supplies the needs of His children and even though it is through faith that we have access to God's grace and favor, total achievement and attainment and full freedom will be only experienced by those who allow the Lord to bring them into maturity.[16] A child of God has great potential to be used of Him if the will is yielded to Him (see John 4:34, 6:38).

One teen I counseled was diagnosed with A.D.D. at the age of eleven, and had been prescribed with Ridilin that she did not take faithfully. She and her mother both had strong wills. The teen however had discovered heterosexuality and became impregnated by another teen with a very unstable background. His mother had been married several times and he did not know his own father. At the beginning of her pregnancy, she was pleased with the fact that she would be able to "control" someone's life instead of being under the authority of her own mother.

The Lord led me to minister to her concerning forgiveness and restoration because a close relative had molested her at a young age after her father had abandoned her mother. As the weeks went by, there was gradual change of heart, but there was still a stronghold in her life that I was discerning. I did not know what it was, so I continued ministering through what I call "prophetic interviewing." Prophetic interviewing is not deductive reasoning; it is a term that describes both God showing a pastoral counselor something revelatory about a person that the counselor would not know unless the Holy Spirit revealed it, coupled with the counselor proceeding in a methodical interview that eventually confirms the revelation from God. In this case, the insight that the Holy Spirit revealed to me was "witchcraft." I gently asked the teen, "Does the word witchcraft relate to you in any way?" "Yeah, my father is a medicine man of a major Indian tribe around here," she replied.

During the following session, with her mother present, I asked her to renounce all unhealthy soul ties between her and her father. I led her in a prayer to also break unhealthy soul ties with her present boyfriend. She was reluctant to do that, so before praying I explained to her, "In order for the fornication to stop, you must release him and yourself from the bonds that have tied you together emotionally. You must allow the word of God and its power to work within you. Let us not let the devil take over your emotions. To keep sinning would be like slapping God in the face. It would be an insult. God loves you and wants you to be whole. I understand your background and the absence of a father or fatherly image, but let's not allow that to be an excuse. You are victorious through the blood of Jesus and His word."

During that session and other sessions in which I was able to *explain* God's plan of restoration for her as an individual, she was very encouraged and challenged to live for Christ. I opened the Bible to her by sharing scriptures such as Psalm 25:7, Ecclesiastes 12:1, Philippians 4:8, First Timothy 4:12 and Second Timothy 2:22, in a spirit of gentleness and meekness (see Gal. 6:1). No one else (even in her church) was willing to do so.

As an objective observer, I saw potential in her. I suggested that she could be a very successful crisis worker someday, (ex. the emergency room of a medical hospital). Toward the end of our sessions she said, "You are the first real Christian I have ever met because you really care about me."

Hyperactivity has also been termed as mania and euphoria by mental health professionals. One thing that people diagnosed with ADD, ADHD, and manic depression (bi-polar disorder) have in common is malfunctioning neuro-transmitters. Yet some Christians tend to think that all causes of these "disorders" are solely demonic. If they were caused only by demonization, then a prayer of deliverance would set them totally free. If they were caused only by behavior problems, then behavior modification would heal them. Nevertheless, I do definitely acknowledge that one *can* benefit from prayers of deliverance, behavior modification, and proper non-addictive medications.

The observation that Dr. Harold Dewberry makes about King David is a good principle to apply to those needing self-control and spiritual healing.

David, in Psalm 42 [author's note: vv.3-4], reveals to us a godly principle that will bring us out of defeat and despair into thankfulness and praise. *'When I remembered these things'* — what things? The things that had caused him to grieve. This word, remember, *'zakar'*, means to recollect, to bring to remembrance, to confess. David remembered (to recall, to recollect, to confess) 'those things', the wrong attitudes that brought him deep depression and inner conflict. He cast these things from his soul. The New Testament would have exhorted him to 'put off' these things from his diseased soul by confessing, for confession brings catharsis, cleansing and healing. More precisely, 'catharsis' means to be made clean from defilement, to be made without spot or wrinkle by a process of purification and purging.[17]

What many people do not realize is that hyperactive children need to be treated spiritually like every other child (see Prov. 22:6; Eph. 6:1; Heb. 12:5-13). The word "train" in Proverbs 22:6 means not only to train up, but also to narrow. The New Testament writer James uses an example of putting bits in horses' mouths — to train them to turn correctly and literally "curb the spirit" in Greek (see 3:3). Horse trainers put blinders on the sides of the eyes of horses so they will not turn to the right or the left. Hyperactive children, if "spiritually curbed", can grow up to be powerful and positive influences in the church.

CHAPTER 13

INTERDEPENDENCE

E. H. Friedman developed a sociological view called the Family System Concept in 1985. It states that each person is interdependent rather than independent. Each component, therefore, rather than having its own distinct identity or input, operates as part of a large whole.[18] This same concept can be seen in Scripture in the early church (see Matt. 14:14-21; Acts 2:41-47; Rom. 12:15; 1 Cor. 12:25-27). We are all functional members of the *body of Christ* in some way if we are in the process of receiving Him into our lives and giving Him out to others.

In ministry to the single population, there are some effective ways we can help them on their journeys with Jesus and others. Though many singles work and go to school, there are constructive ways for them to learn and grow within the corporate body of Christ. Pastoral counselors should encourage singles to fellowship with mature, married couples in small fellowship groups rather than being separated solely into singles only groups. They can encourage them to go on long-term and short-term mission trips or to volunteer for follow-up, benevolence, or hospital visitation ministries. Others may want to be involved with children's ministry (if they do not have molesting histories), wedding coordination, or teaching Sunday school.

Jesus was our prime example of a single person in the Bible. He did not isolate Himself from society, yet He took time out of His busy schedule to rest. Christ's rest became His time of emotional intimacy with His heavenly Father (see Luke 5:15-16, NIV). Jesus often withdrew to be with His Father. The practice of privately withdrawing for prayerful or meditative reasons has been lost for many people today, including busy singles.

Living with oneself is the first step to interdependency. In the Bible, Job lost his children, his servants, his health, and his wealth. His wife was also at odds with him, and loneliness had a prime opportunity to enter his life. Often singles that are not in nurturing families can relate to some aspects of Job's life because there are many opportunities for loneliness to come into their minds and hearts. Yet Job put his confidence in God. He said, "Shall we indeed accept good from God and not accept adversity" (Job 2:10, NAS). Today's singles must do the same.

A courageous young woman, Joni Ericson (Tada), as a preteen had a diving accident that left her paralyzed from the neck down. She matured into single-hood, eventually accepting her physical limitations and who she was as an individual. Joni was not preoccupied with finding a mate. She was occupied with the affairs of Jesus and the calling on her life (see Luke 19:12-17; John 6:26-27) as an artist and minister. I believe when Jesus saw that she was content (see Phil. 4:11; 1 Tim. 6:6), He decided to bless her with the husband of her heart's desire (see Matt. 6:33-34).

Sibling relationships are also part of the family system. We see the first scriptural sibling rivalry in Genesis chapter four, in the account of Cain and Abel. They had differing vocations, and they had two different dispositions. Their resulting outcome was tragic (see Gen. 4:8).

Tamar's life was not happy either. Her half-brother Amnon raped her (see 2 Sam. 13:11-14). About two years later, Tamar's biological brother, Absalom, disobeyed the

Sixth Commandment by murdering his half-brother Amnon (see Ex. 20:13; 2 Sam. 13:28-29). Her story illustrates that when incest occurs in a family, it is difficult to pick up the pieces of sibling unity until many years later, after everyone has become adults.

A common thread in people who have been violated by incest or other molestations is that often the parent(s) does not know about the molester's act. Parent(s) often are oblivious of what is going on with their children, and that often is due to the parent(s) not being healed of his or her own past. King David (and Maacah), Tamar's parents, ignorantly allowed this act to take place by instructing Tamar to go to Amnon's house at a time when Amnon was physically tempted and his hormones were active (see 2 Sam. 13:2,7). This is not to say that the rape was David's fault. Victims, however, must forgive all who were directly and indirectly involved (see Rom. 12:18, 14:19). Through the redemptive power and blood of Christ, all can be healed and live productive lives for the Lord if they face similar situations with hope and forgiveness (see Matt. 19:25-26, 26:28; 2 Cor. 1:3-7).

A Biblical example of positive, interdependent relationships is that of Jesus and His twelve apostles. They had all types of temperaments that are helpful in assisting believers in interdependence.

One of these, Judas Iscariot, was a foreigner, the treasurer of Jesus' ministry, and a betrayer. As we know, eventually he committed suicide. In helping a person like "Judas Iscariot" get connected to the group, a pastoral counselor can make efforts to understand the cultural differences while focusing on the similarities. One could minister the verse from Isaiah that states, "Can a woman forget her sucking child, that she would not have compassion on the son of her womb? Yea, they may forget, yet I will not forget thee. Behold, I have graven thee upon the palms of my hands; thy walls are continually before me" (49:15-16, KJV). Foreigners tend to feel isolated from group interaction and have difficulty with interdependence on people from other cultures or subcultures. Therefore we must minister affirming words to them (see Rom. 15:2), so they will know they are accepted and loved in a social sense (see 1 John 4:7).

Jesus Himself was interdependent upon an inner circle of three disciples — Peter, James, and John. All three were fishermen and had to be interdependent upon others within their "pre-disciple" vocation. James and John came from a family who owned boats and had servants. Peter, interdependent upon his brother Andrew (another disciple), lived in proximity to James and John, and also fished in the Sea of Galilee. The inner circle of Peter, James, and John, along with the other apostles, had much potential because they had many things in common, yet they were also diversified and had a need for interdependence.

Ministers of the Gospel must also learn how to be interdependent upon one another (see Phil. 1:1-7; 1 Thess. 1:1-2). Learning to accept and receive another's gifts without division or competition is vital to furthering the Kingdom of God (see John 17:20-21; Rom. 12:1-18). Furthermore, if someone seeking to be in ministry comes forward, that person must have a desire to work for the betterment of the system as a whole (see Matt.12:25). Teamwork is a vital part of interdependence for both the personal family and the family of God to function to its fullest potential.

CHAPTER 14

JUVENILE PROBLEMS

Flee also youthful lusts: but follow righteousness, faith, charity, peace, with them that call on the Lord out of a pure heart (2 Tim. 2:22, KJV).

It is significant that we encourage the youth to remember the Lord and to fear His name (see Gen. 9:16; Ex. 13:3; 1 Chron. 16:12; Prov. 14:27). The teen years are a time when God often calls people to follow hard after Him and serve Him out of a *pure* heart (Ps. 63:8; 1 Tim. 1:5, 4:12). Obedience to His call can be a deterrent to being involved with the temporary pleasures of sin (Heb. 11:25-26).

Proverb 19:18 states "Discipline your son, for in that there is hope; do not be a willing party to his death" (NIV). Ephesians 6:4 says, "Fathers, do not irritate *and* provoke your children to anger — do not exasperate them to resentment — but rear them [tenderly] in the training *and* discipline and the counsel *and* admonition of the Lord" (AMP, emphasis added). Fathers (and mothers) must tenderly encourage accountability and discipline in rearing their adolescent minor(s). Parental values must be instilled by both example and teaching (see Prov. 22:6; John 13:13-17). "Washing our children's spiritual feet" does not mean bailing them out of jail, doing their laundry, giving them money without earning it, or taking care of the grandchildren born out of wedlock while the teen does not seriously attempt to further him/ herself — in other words, giving them a free ride.

Most of the families I have counseled that involved a pregnant teen have been successful as long as the young woman was given the choice of either placing the baby for adoption or living the rest of her life outside her parents' home. This is difficult advice for the mother of a pregnant teen but important for the marriage of the new-to-be grandparents. The vocation of parenting teens is difficult, but can be positive. We must encourage parents of these teens to rely on the Lord continually for godly wisdom and understanding (see 1 Kings 3:9; Ps. 119:104; Prov. 3:5-6; Acts 17:11; James 1:5).

Teens especially must be encouraged to put down the lusts of the flesh, the lust of the eyes, and the pride of life (1 John 2:15-16), not by parental preaching but by godly love and non-confrontive communication (see 1 Pet. 4:7-8). The prophetic counsel and teaching of the Bible must be administered.

> Now the works of the flesh are manifest, which are these; Adultery, fornication, uncleanness, lasciviousness, idolatry, witchcraft, hatred, variance, emulations, wrath, strife, seditions, heresies, envyings, murders, drunkenness, revelings and such like: of the which I tell you before, as I have also told you in time past that they which do such things shall not inherit the kingdom of God. (Gal. 5:19-21, KJV)

The above verse lists various problem areas, all of which can apply to young people. It will be worth our time to examine each.

1. With adultery meaning disloyalty to one's spouse, an adulterous teenager is one who would have sex with the

future spouse during the courting or formal engagement process. A pastoral counselor with wisdom and discernment would lovingly ask at the right time, "Where are you sexually?" A person gifted in the prophetic may have already heard from the Lord "where they are" sexually. Either way it is up to the counselor to be quick to hear, slow to speak, and slow to anger (see James 1:19). Representatives of Christ (see 2 Cor. 5:20) must exemplify the *phileo* (proprietal) love of God to the preteens and teens that come to their offices for counsel. By doing so, they will be facilitating the salvation of their souls.

2. The English word fornication is both *porneia* and *porneuo* in the Greek; from these Greek words we get the English word pornography. Children and teens are bombarded with semi-pornographic materials from magazines, television, videos, and the Internet inside and outside the home. The answer is not to allow them to see it so that they don't become desensitized. At the same time, parents can give them a healthy respect of both God and the human body by showing love (i.e., kissing) for one another in the home in front of the children.

3. Uncleanness in the Old Testament period mostly referred to religious impurity because there was no blood atonement except by animal sacrifice.

Uncleanness in the New Testament is mentioned eleven times. In ten of these, the word means physically or morally impure. Romans 6:13, 16, and 19 speak about yielding our members as servants to righteousness and holiness. The word "yield" in these verses refers to the Greek word *paristemi* and means to stand beside, i.e., to exhibit or to offer. Pastoral counselors can ask teens, "Are you offering up your body daily to the Lord Jesus (your friend) as a holy and living sacrifice?" (see Rom. 12:1).

It would aid in victory over sins of the flesh if pastoral counselors made Bible memorization a requirement for the teens counseled, due to the truth and validity of such scriptures as, "I have hidden your word in my heart that I might not sin against you" (Ps. 119:11, NIV), and "Thy word is a lamp unto my feet and a light unto my path" (Ps. 119:105, KJV).

4. Lasciviousness (or licentiousness) is an undisciplined and unrestrained behavior, especially a disregard of sexual restraints. It is a New Testament word meaning outrageous conduct, indicating that this behavior goes beyond sin to include disregard for what is right. The spirit of anarchy and lewdness run uncontrolled in the lives of some teenagers and must be confronted with holy boldness through intercessory prayer (see Heb. 4:14-16, 10:18-22).

5. Hard-core idolatry starts at a young age through the power of religion (a false belief system). A clear example of how this works in the natural and spiritual realms is that of Eastern cultures that practice a later form of Taoism. In Taoism, there are many gods to be worshiped by the followers, advocating alchemy, divination, and magic to attain long life and immortality. In many parts of the Far East, *immorality* is widespread. Married and unwed women have had multiple abortions. The cases of exhibitionism and child molestation are innumerable. Not only are false gods idolized, but also so are human bodies. Therefore whoredom (figuratively to commit idolatry) is common practice.

6. Witchcraft has been introduced to children through various role-playing games such as Dungeons and Dragons, Quake, and Tomb Raider. The word witchcraft can have various expressions, such as divination, a divine sentence, to whisper a spell, to enchant, or to practice magic. All the Major Prophets condemned divination.

7. The word "hatred" means hostility, enmity, or a reason for opposition. Many juveniles commit crimes of hate, from defacing property to first-degree murder. We must minister to them in the opposite spirit of the world. Youth must also be taught that hell is a real place and that God will judge all people (see John 5:28-29; 2 Pet. 2:4-12).

8. Variance is the King James Version of the Bible for words such as quarreling, wrangling, contention, debates, and strife. These behaviors usually start in a child's life long before teenage years. The soul of the child must be discerned at a young age before negative verbal fruits have a place to take root. The soul is closely intertwined with the will and moral actions. The soul is capable of stumbling and falling, of abusing freedom and of being led into captivity.[19] Children therefore must be taught to obey and honor their parents within the guidelines of the Bible from an early age to the time they are ready to leave home (see Ex. 20:12; Luke 18:20-21; Eph. 6:1).

Many young Christians have wrongly developed a doctrine from the account of Jonah (the whale and the judgment on Nineveh) as God always being a God of second (third, fourth, and fifth) chances, only to end up contradicting what Christ did on the cross and making it null and void in their lives (see Heb. 6:4-6). We must continue accountability with teenage believers so that they will grow in love and purity (see Ps. 18:21-28; Col. 2:6-7).

9. Though the word "emulations" is only mentioned once in the King James Version of the Bible (Gal. 5:20), it has various meanings such as zeal, indignation, envy, and jealousy. The word comes from the Greek word *zelos,* from which we get other words such as jealous, zealous, zeal, and zealot. Pastoral counselors can encourage the youth to follow after the Lord Jesus with zeal, fierce in the spirit,

envious for the things of Christ rather than the things of the world or the flesh.

10. Wrath, indignation, and fleshly violence are common in teens, especially in those who come from violent or broken homes. The blood of Jesus and the power of His forgiveness must be ministered through the power of His Word (i.e., Eph. 4:31-32; Col. 3:8-10) to these teens that are so easily influenced by their peers and mass media figures.

"Putting on the new man" is the goal for Christian teens before they reach adulthood. They can do this through the process of accountability in a small group and through disciplined personal time with Jesus (see Ps. 86:2-8).

Grace (the divine influence on the heart) must be the target of intercessory prayer for them. Parents must be encouraged to let go of the controlling lifestyle placed on teens by giving them more responsibility with such things as grocery shopping, including them on some family decisions, and encouraging targeted thinking about hypothetical situations that might get them in trouble later.

11. Strife is the fruit of competition. If there is unity on every side, there will be no strife. Yet children are taught in sports to be competitive with others. The Bible says in Second Corinthians,

> For we are not bold to class or compare ourselves with some of those who commend themselves; but when they measure themselves by themselves, and compare themselves with themselves, they are without understanding. But we will not boast beyond our measure, but within the measure of the sphere which God apportioned to us as a measure, to reach even as far as you... But HE WHO BOASTS, LET HIM BOAST IN THE LORD. For not he who

commends himself is approved, but whom the Lord commends. (10:12-13,17-18, NAS, caps added)

Strife first must be conquered within oneself. Then the fruit of peace among the members of Christ will appear. A double-minded, or "dipsuchos", person is one who is torn between carnal and spiritual things.[20] Through continual meditation on Scripture, the mind can be renewed (see Ps. 119:97, 99) and the spirit restored (see 2 Cor. 4:16; Eph. 4:15-24).

Therefore consider the members of your earthly body as dead to immorality, impurity, passion, evil desire, and greed, which amounts to idolatry. For it is on account of these things that the wrath of God will come, and in them you also once walked, when you were living in them. But now you also, put them all aside: anger, wrath, malice, slander, and abusive speech from your mouth. Do not lie to one another, since you laid aside the old self who is being renewed to a true knowledge according to the image of the One who created him. (Col. 3:5-10, NAS)

12. The word "seditions" comes from the Greek word *dichostsis,* which means disunion or dissension. Many teens like to play a "splitting" (manipulative) game with the parents to try to get their own way. In the process, if the parents are not communicating effectively, the teen becomes seditionary until the Holy Spirit convicts the parents and teaches them to be unified in the decisions they make.

A practical way for parents to combat the fruit of sedition is to update each other on their child's latest trends, events, and activities. Ask questions of your spouse like, "Do you want our son (or daughter) to go to the prom?" or "What do you think about allowing our son or daughter to drive the car this Friday night to the ball game?" Come into agreement with one another before the adolescent incites disunity.

13. Heresies are disunions or parties. A "party spirit" would not necessarily be one associated with carousing or revelry in and of itself; rather it is coupled with a spirit of rebellion and anarchy as in the time when Aaron revolted against Moses (see Ex. 32:1-6).

The word "stiff-necked" is used often to describe the people of Israel in the Old Testament, referring to their hardness or stubbornness. Hardness of heart occurs when children are provoked (angered alongside or enraged) by a parent or care giver they love and trust. If parents would lower their tone of voice and look the teenager in the eye, for example, there would be increased obedience as a result (see 1 Cor. 13:5; Eph. 6:4).

14. The issue of "envyings" can also include the sin of covetousness — not being content in the condition or circumstance in which we find ourselves (see Phil. 4:11; 1 Tim. 6:8; Heb. 13:5). Television, shopping, commercials, and magazine ads have been some of the greatest culprits of temptation since the time our children have been toddlers. Therefore it is a wise counselor who asks poignant questions to determine what kind of things are being solicited on television and the Internet so that an appropriate Scripture (see Ps. 101:3, KJV) can be assigned to the teen for memorization in order to develop his or her resistance to Satan (see Matt. 4:1-10).

15. Today, young children and teenagers in Western societies are committing murders. They execute pre-meditated, first degree murders, murders by self-defense, and voluntary and involuntary manslaughter. The word murder

in the Greek, mentioned nine times in the New Testament, is *phonos,* meaning slaughter.

If we interpret the cause for most homicides by the hermeneutical law of first order, we can evaluate Cain as having anger, greed, and/or jealousy toward his brother (see Gen. 4:1-8).

Again, take into account the law of first order concerning suicide. You can see that the counsel of Ahithophel did not go the way he intended (so he could eventually rise to power in Israel). Therefore a motive of selfishness, greed, and probably anger (see 2 Sam. 15:12, 16:21, 17:23) was in his heart. Questions related to committing specific acts such as, "Have you ever thought about using your parent's gun?" or "How would you kill yourself?" would help determine the reality of the situation at hand.

16. Drunkenness is a drugged or deranged condition that results from drinking intoxicating beverages (see Prov. 20:1; 1 Cor. 6:9-11; Eph. 5:18). Medically speaking, a person who is an alcoholic is chemically dependent on the substance of alcohol and may or may not exhibit the more obvious characteristics of a drunkard, such as loud voice tone, violent behavior, and impulsive acts. A biblical explanation of the process of chemical dependency can be found in Proverbs 23:29-35. However, since the problem is more of a physiological one, adolescents would theoretically benefit from education explaining the effects of certain addictive prescription drugs and street drugs and the people who are more susceptible to them. Unfortunately teenagers tend to think, "It won't happen to me."

Furthermore, an adolescent may say that there is no mention of such things as tobacco or marijuana in the Bible in order that they may have permission to sin and rebel. A prayerful, skilled pastoral counselor, sensitive to the voice of the Holy Spirit, can say with a *gentle* but firm voice, "You may bring the judgment of Almighty God upon yourself if you continue in this attitude and behavior".

17. As far as the issue of revelings, the Greek word *komos* is also translated as rioting in Romans 13, which exhorts, "Let us walk honestly, as in the day; not in rioting and drunkenness, not in chambering and wantonness, not in strife and envying. But put on ye the Lord Jesus Christ, and not make provision for the flesh, to fulfill the lusts thereof" (v.13-14, KJV). Youths must practice putting on the new man through prayer, proclamation (of the Word), and praise. *Prison to Praise* by Merlin Carothers would be a good book to have a young person read (see 2 Cor. 6:14-16).

In closing, young people must be saturated in prayer and have parental support through prayer and regular open discussions about these topics so that trust can be both established and maintained between adults and adolescent(s). A suitable intercessory prayer might be, "Father, I come to you in the name of Jesus, the Name above every other name, that every principality and power holding _____ (the person's name), including adultery, fornication, uncleanness, lasciviousness, idolatry, witchcraft, hatred, variance, emulations, wrath, strife, seditions, heresies, envyings, murders, drunkenness, and revelings, must be bound and cast from __ _____. Thank you Father for replacing these foul spirits with Your love, joy, peace, patience, kindness, gentleness, and self-control." A bedside prayer might be, "Thank you Father for _____ (the person's name). Thank you Father for helping _____ to live for You by thinking thoughts that are true, noble, right, pure, lovely, admirable, and excellent, according to Philippians 4:8, and helping me as _____ _____'s parent to be trusting and trustworthy as the main spiritual authority in his (or her) life."

CHAPTER 15

LUST

Current dating principles wrongly allow permissiveness in sexual foreplay. Young people pairing off before they are emotionally, psychologically, or spiritually mature enough to handle their sexual feelings can be easily led to promiscuity.[21]

Lust and promiscuity is often rooted in women who have been sexually molested. While working at a crisis pregnancy center, I would often ask the client if she had been sexually molested as a child. Many responded by affirming the fact and the feeling of guilt and filthiness associated with that experience. The word, "uncleanness", means hurts, bruises, and wounds — the effects of sin. Jesus not only cleanses from all unrighteousness, but also cleanses us from the effects and repercussions of sin. Not only of our own personal sins, but he heals those who are the victims of sin.[22]

In place of lust, the Holy Spirit has the power to produce the fruit of temperance (self-control) in a diligent believer's life (see Gal. 5:22-23 [KJV]). The book of Second Peter speaks about a Christian not having certain divine qualities as "nearsighted." Those who are acting out their lustful passions are not thinking of the welfare of others. While counseling and interceding for a young male inmate at a high security state prison, I discovered through practical questioning that prisoners were receiving pornographic materials through the mail. This young man had

turned to Christ within his first few months at the peniten-
tiary. Yet he was in a dorm with fifty-nine other men. His
description of what was going on behind closed doors was
much like that of a mini-"Sodom and Gomorrah". One night
the Lord came to him in a dream and showed him the evil
spirit that had been upon his family. He described it as being
like that of half man and half beast.

A secular therapist might have thought he was halluci-
nating or approaching a psychotic breakdown, but I know
the demonic realm is real. Through revelation, the Lord
showed me that the spirits of bestiality and lust bound him
and his father's side of the family. So when I met with him,
we prayed to break the generational curses that gave place
to these vexing spirits, back to the third and fourth generation (see Ex. 20:5, 34:7; Num. 14:18). That night he tele-
phoned his parents with the good report. His tone of voice
had changed. The joy of the Lord had strengthened him.

Through more follow-up visits, however, I discovered
that demonic powers had been using other inmates to try
to destroy his new found victory. I encouraged him, "Our
fight is not against flesh and blood, but against principalities,
powers, and wickedness in high places. The devil uses people
for evil purposes. God wants to use you for His purpose and
for furthering His kingdom." I wanted to get more of the
word of God into his life, so I followed-up the visit by asking
the local pastor to send him some teaching tapes on discipleship and the fundamentals of Christianity.

King David gave birth to sin by lusting in his heart
after Bathsheba (see 2 Sam. 11:1-4). In order to correct the
problem, David could have literally walked downstairs, out
from the view of a beautiful woman. Paul, in his letter to the
Galatians, wrote, "But I say, walk and live habitually in the
(Holy) Spirit — responsive to and controlled and guided by
the Spirit; then you will certainly not gratify the cravings and

desires of the flesh — of human nature without God" (5:16, AMP).

Scripturally, lust is basically a longing (usually sexual) for what is forbidden by God. The second letter of Paul to Timothy gives a command and remedy concerning youthful lusts. He says to flee (run away from) youthful lusts, and then pursue (in place of lust) righteousness, faith, love, and peace, along with those who call on the Lord out of a pure heart (see 2:22). Purity is the key to closing the door on such acts as masturbation and pornography. The Greek word here for purity is *katharos*. It is the word from which we get English words such as catheter and catharsis, with purification as the main purpose.

The blood of Jesus and the power of prayer can purge those of us striving for victory over the spirit of lust. David prayed to the Lord after his sin against God, himself, and Bathsheba: "Purify me with hyssop, and I shall be clean [ceremonially]; wash me, and I shall [in reality] be whiter than snow" (Ps. 51:7, AMP). Those who receive the blood atonement of Christ for the forgiveness of sins will be washed. As an individual becomes cleansed by God's power, he or she receives the supernatural love of Christ. No other person or religious institution can offer true love. His love surpasses knowledge (see Eph. 3:18-19). Pastoral counselors must continually pray for their counselees to receive His love, even after they have accepted Christ, because of the wounds and scars that often remain. A wonderful prayer one can use is found in Paul's letter to the church at Ephesus:

I pray that out of his glorious riches he may strengthen you with power through his Spirit in your inner being, so that Christ may dwell in your hearts through faith. And I pray that you, being rooted and established in love, may have power, together with all the saints, to grasp how wide and long and high and deep is the love of Christ, and to know this love that surpasses knowledge — that you may be filled to the measure of all the fullness of God. (3:16-19, NIV)

CHAPTER 16

OBEDIENCE

I know someone who grew up in a denominational church in which her father was a deacon for ten years. In that church, she saw many negative things that unfortunately were hypocritical of true Christianity. As a result, when she came to Christ as a preteen outside that denomination, she became critical of the denomination and thus sowed seeds of discord in her heart. Inward rebellion had set in. A critical attitude was displayed whenever she shared about the spiritual condition of her parents to her Christian friends. However, while in ninth grade, a Christian teacher discerned that the counselee had a judgmental attitude. The teacher was *obedient* to the Lord in telling the student about her problem. The student confessed her sin and was set free from that bondage.

Simple obedience is something all Christians need and must learn. The principle of obedience is taught throughout the word of God. *Hupakouo* is the Greek word commonly translated as "obey" in the New Testament. Its meaning is to listen attentively and to heed or conform to a command or authority.

Believers in Christ must obey governing authorities whether in the church or not (see Rom. 13:1-7; Heb. 13:17). Though we may not always agree with governmental laws, God has chosen that method to protect us physically and legally. This is because human government is a divine institution, instituted by God when Noah came out of the ark. It is a permanent institution for the regulation of human affairs.

During the time I was earning a Masters degree in Marriage, Family, and Child Counseling, I was also teaching four year-olds in a pre-school. One day I was showing a rabbit to the class by kneeling down and leaning into the circle with the animal cupped in my hands. The girl who had been sitting next to me started prodding the crotch of my jeans. I looked back calmly to see which child was prodding me. I did not need revelation from the Holy Spirit to know that something was wrong with this child. She obviously learned the prodding behavior from someone.

After a short time of prayer, I reported the incident to the Child Protection Services. The next day they were at the school investigating. That night the children were safe in another home. The civil court issued a subpoena for me to testify on behalf of the child and the state of California. I went to court with facts in my head and overconfident because I knew I was right. However, when the judge asked me the date and time of day the incident occurred, I became catatonic. I stammered out the wrong time and date of the incident that took place in the classroom, so my testimony was thrown out of the case. As the one who could have defended the child, I was not prepared. One year later, however, a neighbor of the family came to me in church and said, "Dawn, I believe you were right in reporting that incident because I knew something strange was going on in that home."

Obedience can be taught by proper discipline. Hebrews 12:11 says, "All discipline for the moment seems not to be joyful, but sorrowful; yet to those who have been trained by it, afterwards it yields the peaceful fruit of righteousness" (NAS). The Greek word for righteousness is *dikaiosune*. Dikaiosune means equity of character or act. Obedient behavior is easy to do when following a person or leader who is practicing dikaiosune. It is more difficult when the leader is not. Nevertheless, obedience is required of us regardless of what the employer, pastor, or parent is portraying in his or her integrity before the Lord. Dr. Harold Dewberry gives an unfortunate example.

I well remember counseling a middle-aged woman who very reluctantly came to me for ministry. Both her father and a close relative had sexually and emotionally abused her. These "keepers of the wall", the ones entrusted to guard over her emotions and mind, deeply wounded her by betraying this sacred trust. Fear, shame, bitterness and hatred for men became her shield to protect her from further abuse and humiliation.

As a young woman, she had sought counsel from a priest and, much to her amazement and horror he took sexual liberties with her. From this encounter, she developed homosexual tendencies.

After a commitment of her life to Christ, she sought Christian counseling to overcome her homo-sexual tendency. Her marriage had become dysfunc-tional, and her children were turning to rebellion.

Her counselor promised confidentiality, but reported her sexual preference (she had not been involved in any homosexual relationships since conversion) to the pastor of her church. He, instead of allowing love to cover a multitude of sins, publicly denounced her from the pulpit. He condemned her, but he had no answer for her deep cry for deliverance.[23]

I cannot stress enough how much willing obedience is necessary in the pastoral counselor's life. Before one can be an effective pastoral counselor, he or she must be able to hear the word of the Lord for his or her own individual situations.

This means that in order to be used by the Lord in ministry, pastoral counselors must first have active *fellowship* with Jesus that involves effective communication with Him — asking and receiving. Jesus said that if we (Christians) are His sheep, we hear His voice.

In biblical times, slaves were required to be obedient to their masters. Luke 12:47-48 says, "And that slave who knew his master's will and did not get ready or act in accord with his will, shall receive many lashes, but the one who did not know it, and committed deeds worthy of a flogging, will receive but few. And from everyone who has been given much shall much be required; and to whom they entrusted much, of him they will ask all the more" (NAS). Pastoral counselors are not only slaves to Christ as was the Apostle Paul, but have much required of them. The price for carelessness and disobedience cannot be underestimated.

CHAPTER 17

PRAISE

B efore discussing the role of worship in the counseling situation, let's briefly define seven basic Hebrew definitions for worship, taken from the Bible.

Barak means to kneel, to bless, to salute, to praise. Barak is mentioned twice in the Old Testament (Judg. 5:2; Ps. 72:15) and implies quietness before God.

Yadah means to throw out the hands in thankful expression, enjoying God. *Towdah* also means to extend the hands in thanksgiving, and is similar to Yadah. Towdah, however, implies praising the Lord as a sacrifice of praise.

Zamar means to pluck the strings of an instrument, to praise with song (Ps. 47:7, 57:7, 149:3b). *Shabach* means to address in a loud tone, to shout, to triumph, to glory.

Tehiliah means the singing of Halals. The Halals could imply singing hallelujahs to the Lord. Tehiliah is translated thus in Psalms 40:3. Tehillah also means to sing under the anointing of the Holy Spirit. When Jews and Christians tehillah, God inhabits their praise (Ps. 22:3). Tehillah causes a reverence of God to come into one's life (2 Chron. 20:22). Tehillah will build a desire and motivation to praise the Lord (Ps. 71:14).

Halal means to be vigorously excited, to laud, to boast, to shine, to rave, to celebrate, to exalt. Halal implies that the worshiper should love and praise Almighty God with a sense of abandonment. Halal is the most common word for praise in the Bible.

When we praise the Lord, we are thinking more of God and less of ourselves. Praise is an act of worship or acknowledgment by which the virtues or deeds of another are recognized and extolled. When counseling, instead of focusing on the presenting problem that the client gives, I focus on his or her level of fellowship with the Lord. I have often exhorted the counselee to keep the praise of the Lord in the heart and on the lips.

Concerning a specific marriage that was on the verge of divorce, the wife began coming for counsel for her own problem. Eventually the husband began to see positive changes in her life (see 1 Pet. 3:1). For example, instead of just singing in church, she began making melody in her heart at home and praising Jesus. Finally, when the husband came in for counseling, he was ready for personal change, namely becoming closer to Christ and closer to his wife (in that order).

It has been described in some Christian circles that praise is "fast music" and worship is "slow music", as in rhythm or beat. However praise can include traditional hymns as well. Interestingly, one of the most renowned evangelists of our time, Billy Graham, has been heard to say that he reads one psalm and one hymn each morning during his fellowship with the Lord. He is praising the Lord each morning by simply reading or singing a hymn.

There was a time in my life when I ministered for a southern California-based prayer ministry. For one year, I went to my church every Sunday morning at 7:00 a.m. after I left the phone lines. I would attend both services and then spend the entire afternoon with the Lord. I would pray, sing hymns, dance, and worship.

The goal of worship is to focus on God and the things He has done both for us and through us. He has adopted us into

His family whereby we cry out "*Abba.*" *Abba* is an Aramaic word expressing intimacy with and reverence for the Father. *Abba* Father is deserving of our worship because of all the things that He has done.

Pastoral counselors must help the counselee to understand his or her role as a worshiper of *Jesus* the Savior. So many of those who come for counseling need the teaching and the desire to worship the Lord continually.

In pastoral counseling, one incorporates worship in the counseling process by playing worship songs in the office and guiding the counselees into the presence of the Lord. Pastoral counselors should give counselees creative ideas on how to bring worship into their homes and workplaces. They challenge the counselee's worship level to increase in order to increase the healing rate. For teens, pastoral counselors are sensitive yet obedient to ask about the kind of music to which he or she listens.

Much healing is accomplished through music. Music therapists use what is called "music therapy." Physiologically, the right hemisphere of the brain is positively affected by music with or without lyrics. In the world of rock music, there is a certain frequency commonly used. This frequency (in dissonant chords) brings chaos into the mind of the listener because this type of music tries to speak to the left hemisphere of the brain. In Christian and melodic music, the right hemisphere of the brain is correctly affected because the music is congruent to the body part. Thus, a Christian who is being transformed into the image of Jesus Christ must abstain from listening to music that creates confusion within.

When counseling a young Christian in his early twenties, I asked him specifically if he was listening to the local contemporary Christian station. The client said, "sometimes." Immediately I sensed in my spirit that he was keeping the whole truth inside. He was really listening to secular music most of the time. I did not pursue the issue in the counseling process because the Holy Spirit revealed to me that he was not ready for change. The fruit of deception was still in his life and he was not willing for anyone to hold him accountable in discipleship. I purposely gave him some simple homework of both listening to four teaching tapes and increasing his reading of the Bible, knowing he would not complete it. He soon terminated the counseling relationship.

Pastoral counselors must strive for excellence as His mouthpiece (see Prov. 17:27; 1 Pet. 4:11). Their primary purpose is not to minister to others but to minister to the Lord. Pastoral counselors invite Him into the counseling room by giving Him and Him alone the praise due His name (see Matt. 18:20).

CHAPTER 18

QUIETNESS

The preacher of Ecclesiastes says that there is a time to reap and a time to sow, a time to keep silent and a time to speak (Eccl. 3:7). James, a servant of God, wisely exhorts us to be slow to speak, slow to wrath, and quick to hear (1:19). In the counseling process, it is often to our benefit to be quiet, listen to the counselee with our ears, and hear the Holy Spirit with our hearts. Pastoral counselors must be *quiet* in order to hear His voice. This takes a disciplined lifestyle — limited and selective media viewing, music listening, and Internet activity, for example. Being quiet before the Lord, waiting to hear His voice, can be a form of worship, because one is giving the Master his or her undivided attention.

One woman I counseled was losing her father due to cancer. She was convinced by many people who had "heard from God" that her father would not die, but live and declare the works of the Lord. Now I have known many people with cancer, and in only one case did God specifically say, "You will live and not die to declare the works of the Lord." She did not die, but lived to serve the Lord as a foreign missionary. However, the woman who was losing her father was so convinced that he would live that I did not have the heart to tell her what the Lord had revealed to me. I was quiet. Listening was the best ministry I could have given her during that time of increasing grief.

Secular psychotherapy calls the phenomenon of what she was experiencing "denial." Some Christians call it "faith." The revelatory word of the Lord to me said that he would die, but the Holy Spirit also said, "Quiet; be still; you may know the outcome, but hold your peace and minister to her in a spirit of encouragement and joy."

Quietness resulting from remaining silent — not speaking — often is *not* beneficial to the soul. In the culture where my husband and I ministered for four years, the method for social peacemaking was silence, often resulting in chaotic homes, disobedient children, unfaithful spouses, obsessive-compulsive disorders, and psychosomatic illnesses, to name a few. The heart of man is the seat of his affections and interest and from it comes the issues of life. Movement creates measurable energy, and unreleased emotion causes deep inner tension and stress which, in turn, puts pressure on the "sympathetic" part of our memory. When this stress is not released through the proper channels of expression, the physical body reacts.[24]

Unreleased emotion usually equals an inability to communicate feelings verbally in a non-destructive manner. Suppression of the emotions can cause illnesses such as cancer, asthma, skin diseases, and digestive and respiratory problems.

I met a couple that had been missionaries for twenty-five years. She and her husband were sent from a church that believed in the present-day ministry of the gifts of the Holy Spirit. They shared about the power and gifts of the Holy Spirit to other missionaries. After countless rejections from others, the wife became very discouraged, even hopeless. Peace at any price became her only means of emotional survival. After some time, she developed asthma. This was due to her repressed emotions, the rejections, and the isolation. I realized that the asthma could be linked to these many rejections during her early days as a missionary. At that point in the counseling process, it was important to be pastoral because she needed a person who would listen with unconditional love.

When I once ministered for a telephone prayer line as a supervisor, I was made aware that a particular woman was advising physically battered women to obey and submit to their abusive husbands. According to our mission statement, that was not the correct counsel. Instead we sought for these women to become separated from their husbands in order to break the vicious cycle of silence and abuse in their homes.

Often it is the abuser or perpetrator who says after the beating, rape, or perverted act, "And you better not tell anyone (silence, quiet)..." Though the principle of reporting sexual or physical abuse is not recorded in Scripture, obedience to governing authorities is advised (see Rom. 13:1-7) for protection. Good government allows for the reporting of abuse, and protects those who have been harmed.

Sometimes a pastoral word can be, "When was the last time you took a long vacation?" Peace and quiet is difficult to obtain without making quality choices to break away from the demands of this world. "And as for what fell among the thorns, these are [the people] who hear, but as they go on their way they are choked and suffocated with the anxieties and cares and riches and pleasures of life, and their fruit does not ripen — come to maturity and perfection" (Luke 8:14, AMP).

Rest in the minister's life is essential in order to hear from the Lord. In the resting period, the Lord has the opportunity to nourish the personal needs of the minister because busyness has decreased. Sometimes ministers are forced to rest: termination, moral defilement, voluntary resignation, involuntary retirement, or sickness. It is the Lord's desire for the minister to come along side of Him during these times to receive rest for the soul.

While on the foreign mission field, there was a woman who was ambitious and zealous for the things of God. She worked diligently on forming relationships in order to win others to Christ (friendship evangelism). However, the "works" mentality that she had been delivered from ten years prior began to grip her again. A door was also reopened for the root of rejection to bear severe negative fruit to the point of suicidal tendencies. She was so busy in the culture trying to find acceptance that she began to loose sight of God's acceptance of her. Personal devotions and Bible reading came to a standstill. There was no peace, no quietness, and no time to wait on the Lord. Finally two pastors realized her situation and called her off the field for an extended rest period and a time of spiritual renewal (see Is. 40:31).

Jesus desires our undivided attention. Quietness. Silence. Peace. His ear is always there because He is the same yesterday, today, and forever (see Heb. 13:8). He deserves our undivided attention. Pastoral counselors must maintain that precious time with the Lord in order for His ministry to be furthered in their lives.

"For thus saith the Lord GOD, the Holy One of Israel; in returning and rest shall ye be saved; in quietness and confidence shall be your strength..." (Is. 30:15, NKJV).

CHAPTER 19

RESPONDING

A response can be a verbal or a non-verbal reply, while reactions are usually actions done in opposition to another subjectively. In many families, the common form of communication is reacting. Sometimes a chain reaction causes friction from day to day, year to year, and even generation to generation. Blaming and condescending remarks are not godly, and reflect a lack of respect for the person. On the other hand, a healthy relationship is one where each party is mutually satisfied, encouraged, and uplifted. It is one where responses outweigh the reactions.

For the social dynamics of the heterosexual marriage relationship, one can study the Song of Solomon to learn positive and healthy interpersonal responses. In this wonderful book, we find the literature absent of condescending and blaming remarks. For example, "You are altogether beautiful, my darling, and there is no blemish in you" (4:7, NAS), and "How fair and how pleasant you are, O love, with your delights!" (7:6, NKJV).

In pastoral counseling, healthy ways of responding, not reacting, should be taught to the counselees. Sometimes proper *responding* requires a "selah" time. The word *selah* follows many of the Psalms. *Selah* comes from a Hebrew word meaning to pause. Pausing for a long period of time is a good habit to develop, especially when listening to an angry person.

The Bible says that a soft answer turns away wrath (see Prov. 15:1). A soft answer is a tenderhearted answer. Answering with a tender heart requires an attitude of meekness. Both Greek words *praiotes* and *prautes,* used in the New Testament for meekness, imply an attitude of humility. A positive attitude of the heart is vital for effective communication. In Paul's letter to the Ephesians, he exhorts them to, "Be completely humble and gentle; be patient, bearing with one another in love" (4:2, NIV). James writes, "Who is wise and understanding among you? Let him show by his good life his works in meekness of wisdom... But the wisdom from above is first pure, then peaceable, gentle, reasonable, full of mercy..." (James 3:13,17).

In the counseling setting, the pastoral counselor has a wonderful opportunity to be humble, lifting counselees out of the pit by encouraging and reaffirming them as a creation of God.

Pastoral counselors have the ability, through their responses, to encourage faithfulness or unfaithfulness in their clients. Secular and even Christian family therapists sadly have encouraged unfaithfulness to the covenant of marriage for several decades. However, peace at any price is not the true answer. Rather, intercession for the couple and godly wisdom in dealing with the problem must be sought before the question of divorce even arises.

Proverb 17:1 says, "Better a dry crust with peace and quiet than a house full of feasting with strife" (NIV). In a marital case, I gave this Scripture to a husband because volatile communication was part of his lifestyle. I sensed that the Holy Spirit wanted to reveal this proverb to him, but he had never read it before. He almost dismissed the point that the Holy Spirit was trying to make until I explained to him that the Lord was available to him as a listening ear more so than his wife. After weeks of prayer and intercession for the couple, the wife then came in to see me. The first time she came a breakthrough occurred; she admitted to having a problem.

When a counselee responds by admitting to a sin or emotional problem, the battle is half over. During this couple's first session together, she admitted in the presence of her husband that part of the marital conflict was caused by her own unresolved issues. I stopped the session immediately. I asked her to repeat what she had just said so that her husband could hear it again and so that she could hear herself say it again. She had finally begun to *respond.*

CHAPTER 20

TRAINING

During my early twenties, I was increasingly being used by the Holy Spirit in the gift of the word of knowledge as well as in prophetic intercession. One woman in my church was married for the first time at the age of thirty-seven. She and her husband wanted to conceive quickly. She became pregnant soon after marriage. During the pregnancy, she and I prayed regularly for the child within her womb — for health, anointing, and calling. One day the Holy Spirit revealed to me that this child would be a boy. Upon telling the soon-to-be mother, instantly she replied, "The Lord also showed my husband and me that we would have a boy."

The Lord used this word of knowledge to confirm to them His plan and thus give them enough confidence to name the child and to pray over him by name. As she and I began praying for him specifically by name, the child became stronger and more active in her womb. There are also physiological studies that have been done to reinforce the theology of pre-natal care through prayer, singing, and reading aloud the Bible.

This points out the importance of environment as a major factor in the training of a child. God chose for Moses to be reared in Pharaoh's palace, an environment that provided him much of the training that would later be used in his role as the deliverer of the Israelites. Joseph, through the Lord's providence, was placed into Potiphar's family as a slave, where he then became the chief steward over Potiphar's estate. This environment trained him for his God-appointed future role as Pharaoh's "prime minister."

Pastoral counselors are granted the opportunity to contribute new environments to the lives of those who seek their counsel, just as Jesus did. He called several disciples out of an environment of aquatic fishing to one of "fishing" for people.

One of God's major concerns for His people is their development into the image of His Son, Jesus Christ. God gives (spiritual) milk to babes and (spiritual) meat to the mature (see Heb. 5:12-14). In the calling to sonship in Christ, the environment of choice affects the character, a major goal of training.

Dr. Harold Dewberry presents a clear explanation by blending the stages of early childhood with the maturing process in our spiritual development.

> The Greek word, "tecknon", or child is related to "tikto", to beget or bear. It is used both in the natural and the figurative senses, giving prominence to the fact of birth.
>
> "Huios", the word son, is used in the title the Son of God, and primarily signifies the relationship of offspring to parent and not simply the birth, as indicated by "teknon."
>
> The difference between believers as children of God, "teknon", and as sons, "huios", is brought out in Romans 8:14-18.
>
> "Tekna" refers to those who are born of God, while "huios" refers to those who show maturity; who are acting as sons. When referring to the basic relationship as a born again child of God, it is expressed as "tekna."

The word "children" in this reference is "tekna" and is used for a new believer.

When "huios" is used, it gives evidence of the dignity of our relationship and likeness to God's character. An example is used in 1 John 1:3,7.

The expression Son of God, "huios theos", is used of Jesus to manifest His relationship with the Father, or in the expression of His character. The Lord Jesus is never called "teknon theou", a child of God, as believers are.[25]

Pastoral counselors should desire to see each counselee achieve the position of mature Christian sonship. However, they can be assured that virtually everyone who comes into their counseling session has not been effectively trained into the kingdom of God as *huios*. In order to see this happen, then, pastoral counselors must be active in the ministry of discipleship. Counseling provides an excellent opportunity for one-on-one discipleship.

Throughout the many years of Christianity, there have been many methods of discipleship. One of the most effective methods of discipleship is through a friendship or mentor relationship. Likewise, the primary goal of the pastoral counselor must not be to exercise the spiritual gifts of the Holy Spirit, such as prophecy or word of knowledge, but to promote the pastoral gifts of love, compassion, nurturing, guiding, and shepherding so that effective discipleship can take place. Often when one has a prophetic edge in ministry, it is difficult to develop the pastoral side unless one seeks brokenness and humility.

Ethics is an integral part of training. Biblical ethics involves living righteously — doing what is good and refraining from evil (see Is. 33:15-16; Titus 2:12). God's revealed truth about good and evil, not human theories or opinions, is sound.

Seeking God in prayer is necessary in resolving ethical issues because every one is not the same. Each issue is as unique as each person who comes for counseling. The pastoral counselor must be a pray-er, an intercessor, and be able to hear the voice of the Holy Spirit. A life of intercession is not only a requirement for the pastoral counselor for his or her own benefit (see Jude 20) but for the spiritual prosperity of the counselee. The pastoral counselor must pray for the spiritual and emotional healing of each person seen — before and during the sessions.

This issue of ethics includes training in holiness for pastoral counselors. Believers are called to be holy (see Lev. 11:45; 2 Tim. 1:9; 1 Pet. 1:15-16). Holiness is a matter of being set apart for the purposes of God. The Holy Spirit, under the New Covenant, has empowered believers to be set apart by the blood of Jesus positionally and by their conduct experientially (Ps. 4:3; Eph. 2:10; Titus 2:14; James 2:24).

Jesus' ethical teaching included the beatitudes at the Sermon on the Mount, recorded in chapters five through seven in the book of Matthew. We are reminded by this teaching that grace comes before His commands (see Matt. 5:3-12) and that His commands are not grievous or burdensome (see 1 John 5:3). Essentially it is our ethical duty to love our neighbor, both socially and morally. We would even do well if we approached our fellow man as if we were to die tomorrow, facing the judgment seat of Christ! Furthermore keeping short accounts with God and man is ethically vital in being equipped for every good work. In the training process, one must be striving for a harmonious relationship with Christ and with man.

Training must include personal healing of self-inflicted and family-related wounds. Wounded people in the church must seek healing before bitterness and resentment take root. This is even true of the pastoral counselor. Walking in humility is a major key to seeing this occur.

Careful thought and contemplation, not impulsivity, is part of the necessary training for the pastoral counselor. When one is accustomed to hearing or sensing the Holy Spirit's voice, it can become easy and quick to deliver the appropriate counsel. One must remember, however, that patience is a fruit of the Holy Spirit and thus part of the Christian character (see 2 Cor. 6:4-10; Gal. 5:22; Eph. 4:2-3).

The pastoral counselor's method for replenishment is spending time consistently in the presence of *Abba* Father. Psalm 42:1 says, "As the deer pants and longs for the water brooks, so I pant and long for you, O God" (AMP). A deer is known to drink from a water source hourly. Keeping the mind stayed on Him will not only give one perfect peace, but will allow one to walk in the Holy Spirit (see Is. 26:3; Gal. 5:16-18,25).

CHAPTER 21

UNDERSTANDING

Pastoral counselors need an understanding heart in order to minister with compassion to the flock of Jesus Christ. They must pray, as Solomon did, for an understanding heart in order to distinguish between right and wrong and to "govern" the people (see 1 Kings 3:9).

> Because you have asked this, and have not asked for long life, or for riches, or for the life of your enemies, but have asked for yourself understanding to recognize what is just and right, Behold, I have done as you asked. I have given you a wise, discerning mind... (1 Kings 3:11-12a, AMP).

An understanding heart involves knowing the plan of God. "'All this', said David, 'the LORD made me understand in writing by his hand upon me, even all the works of this pattern'" (1 Chron. 28:19, KJV). Pastoral counselors must have the goal of finding a "tabernacle" for God within the counselee. The key is understanding Christ's goal for that person rather than all the minute details of the person's past history. Historical knowledge is good for research and diagnosis up to a point, but can sometimes hinder the ability to hear prophetically and pastorally the mind of the Lord concerning the counselee. The pastoral counselor needs to hear the word of the Lord that is meaningful to the situation and minister it.

Once a businessman came to my home. He explained about his business and gave me his business card. I asked him if he went to church, naming a certain denomination in the question. The answer was affirmative. As the Holy Spirit prompted, I said, "You don't go regularly do you?" He said, "No." The Lord prompted me further to ask, "You need to read your Bible more." He replied positively with a new fear of the Lord in his heart.

Testing is a necessary part of the formation of understanding. "And thou shalt remember all the way which the LORD thy God led thee these forty years in the wilderness, to humble thee, and to prove thee, to know what was in thine heart, whether thou wouldest keep his commands, or no" (Deut. 8:2, KJV). Paul had these words to say, "I am not commanding you, but I want to test the sincerity of your love by comparing it with the earnestness of others" (2 Cor. 8:8, NIV). Peter writes, "So that [the genuineness] of your faith may be tested, [your faith] which is infinitely more precious than the perishable gold which is tested and purified by fire. [This proving of your faith is intended] to rebound to [your] praise and glory and honor when Jesus Christ, the Messiah, the Anointed One, is revealed" (1 Pet. 1:7, AMP). A person who has been tested thoroughly will have the fruits of godly love and a pure attitude.

Dr. Harold Dewberry adds to the aspect of proving.

A godly perspective and right attitude of heart are basic requirements for creating unity. The correct pastoral purpose is to produce fellowship and the strengthening, consoling and encouraging of relationships through deep affection and compassionate sympathy.

To do this we must develop a servant's heart.

Paul, in Philippians, states that our attitude should be like that which was shown to us by Jesus Christ, who, though being essentially one with God and in the form of God, did not think that this equality was a thing to be grasped or retained. He laid aside His mighty power and became like men.

As we study the Word of God we see a vast difference between those who seek authority for the purpose of ruling over others and those who function in authority according to the principles set out in biblical philosophy.[26]

Jesus teaches through His own words.

And Jesus called them to Him and said, You know that the rulers of the Gentiles lord it over them, and their great men hold them in subjection, tyrannizing over them. Not so shall it be among you; but whoever wishes to be great among you must be your servant, and whoever desires to be first among you must be your slave; just as the Son of man came not to be waited on but to serve, and to give His life as a ransom for many — the price paid to set them free (Matt. 20:25-28, AMP).

Servanthood is both by choice and by calling. The call as a pastoral counselor requires serving. The pastoral part of pastoral counseling is one of service and commitment. "Washing the feet" of every counselee is the unattainable goal that nevertheless one must strive to obtain, seeking to be more like Jesus each day, being changed from glory to glory into His beautiful image, so that one can shine forth His love, understanding, and compassion to others while being the salt of the earth. One must not fall into the trap of selfishness as did the shepherds of Ezekiel chapter thirty-four.

Rather one must continually seek to be cast into the mold of Jesus Christ, empowered by the Holy Spirit to love and serve others. Without Him, one really cannot do anything fruitful.

In order to be a fruitful counselor, one must follow the Holy Spirit and use His gifts wisely. An aspect of counseling is giving objective, godly advice. The Pharisees and lawyers did not receive the godly type of counsel, nor did they give it (see Luke 7:30). Yet counseling *is* for the people of God, to be healed and to have a closer walk with Jesus Christ. "Just a closer walk with Thee, grant it Jesus is my plea, daily walking close to Thee, let it be, dear Lord, let it be" must be the cry of the counselor's heart for the counselees.

One woman whom I counseled had three abortions before marriage to her present husband. She was bi-cultural. Her mother's side of the family came from a country that allowed exhibitionism with children and practiced abortion as *the* form of birth control. The counselee had been bathed nightly with her mother until the age of ten. Her mother also had multiple abortions.

The counselee, through the course of counseling, became pregnant. Keep in mind that she had been a born again Christian for several years prior to counseling. She confided to me, "I really don't want this baby. It would be so much easier to get an abortion." I explained to her that she was under a generational and cultural curse. She was not aware of the widespread practice of abortion in her mother's country where the counselee had lived for only two years of her life. A resolution to her (and her husband's) problem came when every aspect of her situation was carefully considered. She ended up keeping the baby, their third child and firstborn son.

Biblically one must recognize the Great Counselor, the Holy Spirit, guiding the counselee into His truth through the pastoral counselor (see John 16:13). To gain more understanding into people's lives, one must ask the Holy Spirit for wisdom, meditate on God's Holy Word, and experience life's trials.

"I was young and now I am old, yet I have never seen the righteous forsaken nor their children begging bread" (Ps. 37:25, NIV). That is the experience of understanding.

CHAPTER 22

VEXATION

A person is often vexed when he or she loses hope and starts thinking in a downward spiral pattern. Depression commonly follows. This kind of vexation usually starts with negative thoughts and feelings toward self that must be dealt with.

One woman I counseled was plagued with thoughts of worthlessness and despair. The Holy Spirit revealed to me that there was a secret sin involved in her past, but I did not know the specific kind. Later, when trust had been established, she brought forth a journal in which she had been writing many things about her past. The writings revealed that she had been repeatedly molested by her father (incest). In turn she had resorted to bestiality for further gratification. All of this resulted in her becoming a victim of subconscious guilt. Dr. Harold Dewberry gives some important insight into subconscious guilt.

Subconscious guilt is caused by the removal of the incident from conscious thought patterns by trauma, rationalization, blame shifting, shock, drugs or hypno-therapy.

A person can remove guilt from the conscious mind by the above methods, but the guilt will remain in the subconscious area, causing fear, anxiety, depression, anger. Many times, because of the emotional energy which is created, it will manifest itself through psychosomatic illness or abnormal behavioral traits.

The deadening, or searing, of the conscience leads men to become reprobate. That state will cause men to give themselves over to all manner of uncleanness while others become spiritual shipwrecks.[27]

This woman had become a man-hater as a result of the acts of incest inflicted upon her. Vexation of her mind became a way of life because she was not able to verbalize the incidents to someone she trusted. Hard rock music had become part of her lifestyle. The television was constantly tuned in to trivial shows, dramas, or talk shows. She was not filling her mind with the knowledge of Christ but with the knowledge of the world. Her two year-old, desperately needing to see a godly example in his parents' lives, was being influenced by this demonic environment,.

Her case required high maintenance — much intercession and spiritual warfare. My prayer was, "Loving Heavenly Father, I bow in worship and praise before you. My sister is covered with the blood of the Lord Jesus as her protection. I pray that she is totally and unreservedly surrendered to you in every area of her life. I intercede for her against all the workings of Satan that hinder her. Satan, I command you in the name of the Lord Jesus Christ to leave my sister. I resist on her behalf all of your endeavors to rob her of the will of God. Lord Jesus, let her be transformed by the renewing of her mind in Your mighty name."

As the counseling relationship continued, her trust level toward both men and God grew. She began to fulfill her role as an emotional support for her husband.

Vexation can cause all kinds of self-destructive behavior if the person either is obsessed with negative thoughts toward self or is tormented with thoughts the devil puts into his or her mind. Thoughts of worthlessness must be counteracted with thoughts of righteousness. The pastoral counselor, with the guidance of the Holy Spirit, can ask the counselee about his or her thought processes, such as, "What kind of thoughts are repeated in your mind daily?"

I counseled one man whose meditation was constantly the word of God (he quoted it well), but he was also "meditating" on pretty women each time he would see one. This man had been both married and divorced twice. He was vexed by both an unclean spirit and loneliness. The Lord Jesus loved that man, but He did not love his sins of lust and masturbation. The Holy Spirit led me to read to him Hebrews 10:26, which states, "For if we go on deliberately sinning after once acquiring the knowledge of the truth, there is no longer any sacrifice left to atone for [our] sins —no further offering to which to look forward" (AMP). He irreverently said, "That is the one verse I hate in the whole Bible." He never was repentant. When I realized he also saw me as an attractive woman, I terminated the counseling sessions and gave his situation to the Lord.

Through prayer and the power of the Holy Spirit, the root of demonic vexation is uprooted. It is rendered powerless.

One day I was meditating on the biblical story of the healing of the daughter of the woman of Canaan. This young girl was grievously vexed with a demon. As I continued to ponder this, understanding began to come as I realized that I had always regarded an unclean spirit as a spirit causing immoral sexual behavior. Then I turned to Matthew 12:43-45.

When the unclean spirit is gone out of a man, he walketh through dry places, seeking rest and findeth none. Then he saith; "I will return into my house from whence I came out", and when he is come, he findeth it empty, swept, and garnished. Then goeth he, and taketh with himself seven other spirits more wicked than himself, and they enter in and dwell there: and the last state of that man is worse than the first... (KJV).

Jesus said that when the unclean spirit leaves a person, it walks through dry places, seeking rest. Finding none, it attempts to return to the person who had been cleaned up yet remained unoccupied. Many people have suffered from deep personal rejection; others, because of an inability to face conflict, have withdrawn into isolation and deep loneliness. Yet there is one thing in common — all feel a vacuum, an emptiness within, and a sense of internal isolation.

Oftentimes, we think that a person must be living an immoral life to be vexed by an unclean spirit. But I am convinced that unclean spirits may vex because of the emptiness, the vacuums, and the unfilled needs within. Manifestations of unclean spirits can sometimes appear through severe forms of physical sickness. Other manifestations are emotional and mental torments, such as anger, hostility, and contentiousness.

As pastoral counselors minister to those who need healing, they must be very discerning in order to pray effectively for release and restoration. Pastoral counselors are called to intercede in prayer for the counselee and fight against any satanic vexation. If the counselor would spend as much time in prayer as he or she does in the counseling room, then there would be better results. Each time I have personally bathed the counselee's situation in prayer and praise, I have seen a counselee set free and delivered more thoroughly than when I have merely counseled by my intellectual reasoning and experience.

CHAPTER 23

WHOLENESS

A s a teenager, I led to Christ a fellow teen who was an all-star athlete and desired to be a fashion model. She thought wholeness was in her physical being only. Her father reinforced this idea by demanding that she stay at a low body weight. She struggled with feeling love and acceptance as a young woman. She was compelled to "perform" to get love from significant others; she was not whole in her soul. I knew that Christ was the answer to her deep need. The young woman received Christ into her heart, started reading the Bible, and began attending campus Bible studies. She was on her way to wholeness.

There are several theological schools of thought about how the spirit, soul, and body are divided. J. Rodman Williams, in his three-part volume on *Renewal Theology,* explains.

The soul can be spoken of as the inner life of man through which the spirit expresses itself. Man is a living and conscious soul, or self, as demonstrated in the wide range of his intellectual, emotional, and volitional activity. Accordingly, mind, feeling, and will are all aspects of the soul in action. With the incursion of sin there has been a darkening of the soul, indeed a turning from God in all these vital areas. As salvation has been received, the mind is able again to ponder the things of God, the emotions to sense and enjoy the presence of God, the will to move in harmony with God's purposes. Yet the soul needs further cleansing and strengthening.[28]

A primary role of the pastoral counselor is to facilitate greater cleansing and strengthening of the soul. We can safely say that the soul, the *psuche* in Greek, is comprised of the mind, the emotions, and the will. More important than the technical divisions of the soul, however, is the technique used in ministry to a hurting soul. Through continued personal interaction under the direction and anointing of the Holy Spirit, we endeavor to bring healing to the damaged emotions and to the painful, delusive or re-awakened mind and consciousness. The inner personality, or the soul, would then be restored. The pastoral care and counseling ministry is to ultimately lead the Christian who is oppressed or in bondage into victory and the establishment of inner tranquility and peace.[29]

Before a pastoral counselor can minister to others, he or she must have a certain degree of wholeness him/herself. This includes knowing the limitations of self. Many counselors have gone forth into ministry only to suffer "burn out" years later. An interpretation for burn out can be "not relying on God's grace to carry situations." If a person is not relying on God's grace, he or she is relying on self. Self-reliance must be confronted. This includes any tendency to talk too much about one's accomplishments in ministry. One must be careful to give God the praise and glory for these things. Let he or she who boasts, boast in the Lord (see 2 Cor. 10:17).

I know a person who had been in a local church for most of her life. She was under a nurturing leadership who recognized her prophetic gifts. When she became an adult, she started working part time for an international ministry. While in college, this young lady was also quite active in Campus Crusade for Christ. Her experience in ministry coupled with the gifts that she *knew* she had due to the continual affirmation of these gifts created a spiritual pride within her. At the time, however, she did not know that in the distant future she was going to undergo a humbling experience.

She went into full-time ministry, yet after four years the Lord brought her into a place of humility through an illness that had no cure. It required medical intervention through ongoing psychiatric treatment, something she had "proudly" preached against for years to many who had come to her for prayer. Eventually she resigned herself to the fact that she, although believing in divine healing, would be on medication for the rest of her life.

This is to say that wholeness involves not only recognizing the needs in others and helping them in those needs, but it also includes seeing and correcting the weak areas in one's own life. Again, before a pastoral counselor can assist others in being whole, he or she must be whole.

A whole person will see beauty in everyone. Hence, a whole pastoral counselor may see something negative in the counselee, but will always find something positive to displace the negative in order for the counselee to become more whole.

Obedience is part of the lifestyle of the whole Christian and thus the whole pastoral counselor. A person walking the road of obedience is whole if he or she is not turning to the right or the left of the narrow path toward Christlikeness and is relying on the Holy Spirit to empower him or her.

With obedience as part of the whole person's lifestyle, quietness and confidence will result. Pastoral counselors will not be anxious about crisis situations of any kind, but will go to God and *receive* the peace and quietness of the Lord.

Finally, the whole pastoral counselor allows the Holy Spirit to lead him or her in responding, not reacting, to the problems of the counselee. In turn, the counselor is calm and compassionate in the counseling sessions. The pastoral counselor then knows how to respond with stability in crisis situations, family dilemmas, and typical pastoral concerns, guided by the Holy Spirit.

CHAPTER 24

YIELDING

The yielding to family needs by pastoral counselors can be one of the most difficult goals to accomplish and can become nearly impossible without purposing daily to spend some time with one's family members. Pastoral counselors must be servants of the Lord to their families first, then to their counselees. "Those who have served well gain an excellent standing and great assurance in their faith in Christ Jesus" (1 Tim. 3:13, NIV). "Serving well" is a characteristic of a skilled pastoral counselor.

In addition, receiving corrective, exhortative, and encouraging words from others is something a pastoral counselor must do throughout his or her ministry in order to both stay refreshed and continually give out. Receiving in this regard is part of the yielding concept, since a yielded counselor is giving, and one cannot give more than he or she has received. Many in ministry have wrongly yielded to the "Messiah Complex" mentality which says, "I can do everything for everybody because I have the Spirit of Christ in me", basing this thinking on the Scripture which says, "I can do all things through Christ who strengthens me." The word of God is true in Philippians 4:13. However, it must be balanced with Scripture such as John 1:16 and First Corinthians 15:10.

A pastoral counselor will be prompted by the Holy Spirit in the counseling session to express godly motives to the counselee in order to establish trust. In working with teens, it is easier for them to see heartfelt motives without many words because they are usually transparent. Adults, on the other hand, can be difficult to establish interrelational trust. Yielding therefore to the fruit of patience is necessary in these situations.

Pastoral counselors are to be peacemakers while telling the truth in love, which may at times seem to inflict pain, but is purposed to heal in the long run. Jesus was yielded to his Father to speak His words of truth in order to set people free. Though He may have been concerned about people's emotions (see Matt. 8:26; Luke 24:38), He was not yielded to the manipulation of them. Likewise, when the pastoral counselor is faced with issues related to obedience, he or she must choose life and guide others in choosing life. This requires the pastoral counselor to be yielded to the Great Commission, convicted that the restoration of souls can only be completed through the personal acceptance of Jesus Christ and His shed blood for the forgiveness of sins. Therefore a pastoral counselor yields fruit that will lead a soul into salvation.

Nothing is impossible with God. He can heal and cure every person without the pastoral counselor's help. He wants to use pastoral counselors, but He does not need to. He has the primary, final, and complete healing touch. No one and nothing is greater than the Great Pastoral Counselor, the Holy Spirit. Above all, the human pastoral counselor must be yielded to Him.

FOOTNOTES

[1] Broger, John C., *Self Confrontation,* Lesson 20, p. 2, Thomas Nelson Publishers, Nashville, Tennessee, 1994

[2] Dewberry, Ph.D., Harold R., *Feed My Sheep Feed My Lambs,* p. 60, New Wine Press, Chichester, England, 1995

[3] Broger, John C., *Self Confrontation,* Lesson 11, p. 1, Thomas Nelson Publishers, Nashville, Tennessee, 1994

[4] Dewberry, Ph.D., Harold R., *Feed My Sheep Feed My Lambs,* p. 202, New Wine Press, Chichester, England, 1995

[5] The Random House Dictionary of the English Language, College Edition, Random House, New York, New York, 1969

[6] Dewberry, Ph.D., Harold R., *Feed My Sheep Feed My Lambs,* p. 132, New Wine Press, Chichester, England, 1995

[7] Ibid, p. 136

[8] Ibid, pp. 113

[9] Ibid, p. 71

[10] Ibid, p. 284

[11] Ibid, pp. 143-144

[12] Ibid, p. 176

[13] Ibid, p. 209

[14] Ibid, p. 184

[15] Ibid, p. 224

[16] Ibid, p. 25

[17] Ibid, p. 147

[18] Ibid, p. 37

[19] Ibid, p. 51

[20] Ibid, p. 159

[21] Ibid, p. 221

[22] Ibid, p. 185

[23] Ibid, p. 33-34

[24] Ibid, p. 98

[25] Ibid, pp. 171-172

[26] Ibid, pp. 67-68

[27] Ibid, p. 202

[28] Williams, J. Rodman, *Renewal Theology*, Vol. II, pp. 95-96, Zondervan Publishing House, Grand Rapids, Michigan, 1990

[29] Dewberry, Ph.D., Harold R., *Feed My Sheep Feed My Lambs*, p. 50, New Wine Press, Chichester, England, 1985

Printed in the United States
140501LV00002B/4/A